Emails From A Nut

E. J. PITTMAN
&
JACKSON SNEAD

Illustrated by
MIKE LAING

Note for Librarians: A cataloguing record for this book is available from Library and Archives
Canada at www.collectionscanada.ca/amicus/index-e.html
ISBN 1-4120-8444-X

Book design by
Eric Pittman and Mike Laing

*Printed in Victoria, BC, Canada. Printed on paper with minimum 30% recycled fibre.
Trafford's print shop runs on "green energy" from solar, wind and other environmentally-friendly power sources.*

Offices in Canada, USA, Ireland and UK

Book sales for North America and international:
Trafford Publishing, 6E–2333 Government St.,
Victoria, BC V8T 4P4 CANADA
phone 250 383 6864 (toll-free 1 888 232 4444)
fax 250 383 6804; email to orders@trafford.com
Book sales in Europe:
Trafford Publishing (UK) Limited, 9 Park End Street, 2nd Floor
Oxford, UK OX1 1HH UNITED KINGDOM
phone 44 (0)1865 722 113 (local rate 0845 230 9601)
facsimile 44 (0)1865 722 868; info.uk@trafford.com
Order online at:
trafford.com/06-0199

10 9 8 7 6 5 4 3

FOREWORD

Approved (not written) by Arthur Black

(*Sometimes you just have to read between the lines*)

From: Eric Pittman
To: Arthur Black
Sent: Tuesday July 25 2006
Subject: Submitted for your approval from the
Twilight Zone

Dear Arthur,
I know how busy you are, given the projects you are involved with, so I submit the following for your approval. You may just want to read the alternating bold lines or the whole thing, depending on your mood.

Dear Readers,

Regarding E.J.Pittman and Jackson Snead:

I have struggled to hold myself back from taking the

book to my publisher, grabbing the

law into my own hands and

putting my own name on it. I also thought of

busting up this guy's computer.

However, since I draw strength from other's humor and

I have been bombarded by requests to

write funny stuff over the years, I find this an inspirational volume. I also

participate in all kinds of weird and wacky things.

But certainly none which hold a candle to this guy. Except this little episode;

If he had his way, I would have appeared at a gathering of

writers to read from his hilarious works. Instead I went to a meeting of

the Survivors of Gastro Effluvium Disorder group on board a BC Ferry and

it was a disastrous event so I decided to leave early. I

placed my head through a life ring to

keep my head above water while I leapt off the ferry. My departure caused the ferry to

deliver a punchline which consisted of "Toot, Toot".

Amid the chaos that ensued, the captain threatened me with arrest.

When I declined that offer, he requested that I merely reply with an email which said

I was alive and well following my swim to shore. I also replied to the ferry with my own,

"Toot Toot". Later he claimed to have some kind of

problem with the steering mechanism and BC Ferries took

subversive control of my credit cards and insisted

I pay for the ferry repairs with a huge bill on VISA. VISA also claims

I put on a diving suit to watch an underwater play, "Squid of LaMancha".

According to VISA's collection team, I am now in their lawyer's book about weird Canadian writers.

Then he has the gall to ask for a foreword to his book.

There were accusations back and forth until the lawyer offered to settle for a "sorry" note.

When I decline to write this little piece, he sends me his own version and asks me to

sign it, so that it can be included in his book. People like this will even

tell you what lines to read to gain a sense of the book. My experience of this

tells me that I may not have seen the end of it yet, and this

guy's correspondence has been confusing, frustrating, bizarre, and

very persuasive. I find myself wondering if I should meet him, which is sad and

sometimes funny. Luckily, E.J. Pittman and Jackson Snead are just harmless nuts, but

my old dog is on alert and I'm thinking of moving. I'm too old to be jumping off ferries anyway and

I may have to change my email address. Somebody call the police.

REPLY

From: Arthur Black
To: Eric Pittman
Sent: Thursday, July 27, 2006
Subject: Re: Submitted for your approval
from the twilight zone

Eric, this is wonderful. We don't deserve you, lad. Publish, with my blessing.

Arthur (Pius XIII)

INTRODUCTION
THE MYTH OF JACKSON SNEAD

I have known Jackson Snead since I was about 5 years old. We went to school together in Halifax after his foster parents gave up the prairies for a lobster boat in Nova Scotia. We were fairly close during those years and he confided many times that he had a burning desire to find his biological parents and family. All he had to go on were a few handwritten notes detailing his family's occupation as animal trainers which were tucked in his shorts when he was first dropped off at the Winnipeg orphanage.

After high school, he decided to leave Nova Scotia declaring that he wanted to find his parents and roots.

The next time I saw him, I was doing a geological survey of Northern Saskatchewan near Uranium City. I returned to my cabin one day to find him plucking a ptarmigan and stoking the stove in preparation for dinner.

At that time, he told me this incredible story about how he had been chased by a polar bear near Churchill, Manitoba and had kept running till he got to this cabin. He was quite skinny and nervous and although I was skeptical of his story, I welcomed him to stay, happy to have some familiar human company.

Throughout that summer, he proved to be an entertaining and capable companion, gathering fresh meat during the day and at night telling wild stories which, after some sober reflection and without the influence of lonely bush life, seem a little far fetched.

Through his research into his roots, he claimed to have originally been born in one of the Slavic countries and brought to Canada by his family while on an expedition to recruit dancing bears for their circus act. Apparently they had left him behind during a particularly hasty departure.

He has a tattoo of a camel in a circle with a slash across it on his buttocks, which he claims to be his family insignia and the mark of royal entertainers.

At the end of the summer, he departed to continue his search. I did not see, hear, or think of him for many years until I was on a tour of Kenya and I ran into him on a back country trail. This time, he claimed to be on the run from a warlord's hired guns after some kind of business disagreement. Unfortunately, I was unable to give him safe harbor, and he fled into the jungle and disappeared. I thought that was the last time I would ever see him.

It was some years later when a friend in New Zealand sent me a copy of a local newspaper article that I heard of him again. This time he surfaced as the Living God of a Cargo Cult on the small island of Pomeratu in the South Pacific. Again, the story seemed a little too fantastic to believe. He spun a tale detailing his jungle adventures and his escape from Kenya in an amphibious landing craft which he had commandeered from an army compound.

He claims to have run out of fuel far from shore and drifted for weeks or months before being washed ashore on Pomeratu and mistaken as the Cargo God that the cult had been praying for. He was then worshipped and treated as a deity among the natives for quite some time.

Jackson seemed to have found his perfect place until his miracle making abilities ran a bit shy of the native's requirements for their living god. The islanders eventually voted for a change and through the most unlikely of events, Jackson found himself adrift on the Pacific again. Then, many weeks later, he washed ashore on Long Beach near Tofino, Vancouver Island, where he lived with the squatters and surfers till the end of the summer.

Our paths crossed again when I picked him up hitchhiking and gave him a ride to Victoria.

Again his tales of adventure stretched credibility, but for pure entertainment value and curiosity, I allowed him to stay in a trailer that I had parked in my driveway until he got on his feet.

He spent many months secluded and working on his computer until one day he vanished. When I went to investigate the empty trailer, I found a stash of letters and photographs with a note giving them to me.

He said he was off to open a mobile chicken restaurant in a double-decker bus and pledged to travel the continent while searching for more clues about his heritage.

He asked that I publish these letters and hopefully, it would attract the attention of someone who knew his family. Meanwhile, he continues his search through the highways and back roads of North America.

Supposedly, his bus is called the Cluck 'N Pluck Mobile Chicken Restaurant and will be coming to a country fair near you soon. He hopes to have the Kentucky Fried Chicken recipe and affiliation soon.

At least, that's what I'd like you to believe.

E. J. Pittman

MANY THANKS TO:
Mike, Mike, Jane, Dave, Paula, Darren,
Bjorn, Bill, Arthur, Ryan, Cherie, Kay,
Derek, Rochelle, Alex, Max,
and Monkey Boy

100% Genuine Real Authentic E-mails and Responses

CONTENTS

Volkswagen: Driver Wanted, Driver Found......................................1

Cover Girl Cosmetics: Cover Guy......................................5

Calgary Flames: Hockey Highlights for Men..........................10

Safeway Stores: Bagless Bob...13

Greyhound Bus Lines: A Ticket to Ride..............................19

London School Of Business: Swimming With Sharks................22

Starbucks: Special Coffee..24

Lee Valley Tools: Duct Tape..38

Weekly World News: Cargo Cult God..................................46

Florsheim Shoes: Walker Texas Mouse-Killer.........................53

Imperial Tobacco: Cigarette Detective.............................68

VISA: Vancouver Island Separatist Association......................83

Pamela Anderson: Pam for Premier...................................93

BC Ferries: Freedom Ferry..95

Guinness Book Of Records: A New World Record.......................108

Grandma Susie: My Dilemma...111

Vancouver Aquarium: I'd Like to Donate My Squid...................113

Buffalo Ensemble Theatre: Booking Your Theatre....................120

Island Windows: We Need Special Windows...........................122

Pi55 Beer: Fountain of Youth.......................................124

M&M Meats: We Need Specialty Meats.......................130

Dr. Magic Box: Test My Potato................................135

Sex Shop Canada: Benjamin Bunny Needs a Sex Toy...................145

Tim Horton's: Coffee Cup Conservation.....................153

NASA: Plan Eight for Pluto...................................157

Priceline.com: Holiday Hobo...............................161

Kentucky Fried Chicken:
Cluck 'N Pluck Mobile Chicken Restaurant.......................167

Bear Mountain Resort: Naked Golfing......................170

Enquiry BC: Who Do I Report This To?......................173

BC Ministry Of Environment: My Brother is a Bigfoot.............174

BC Premiers Office: My Brother is a Bigfoot..............177

Santa Claus: My Brother is a Bigfoot......................180

Andorran Embassy: I'd Like to Join the Olympic Team..............182

Lee Valley Tools: Stud Finder..............................185

ESSO: Pump Me Up...187

Ducks Unlimited: Stop The Fence!..........................192

Labatts: Beer's Best Friend.................................194

City Conference Center:
International Association of Indoor Aquarium Farmers.........197

VOLKSWAGEN

DRIVER WANTED, DRIVER FOUND

From: Jackson Snead
To: Volkswagen
Sent: Saturday, August 2, 2003
Subject: Driver Wanted, Driver Found

Dear Volksen-folksen,

I love to drive. I really, really love it!! I once drove from Victoria to Las Vegas in 24 hours nonstop. I only peed once going through Bakersfield. (I lost a little time there because of the clean up) But otherwise, it might have been some kind of driving record.

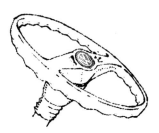

There is just something about moving down an asphalt ribbon away from a town to a new horizon. I have always owned Volkswagens too. My first car was a convertible Karman Ghia.

I had that till the seats got pushed through the roof by a hoist in a Nova Scotia garage. Then I got a beetle. I was hip. Then I got a VW Van. I rocked. I even lived in the van for a while. (Postal code: VnB-RkN , get it?)

So I've been seeing your ads for a long time searching for drivers and I finally decided that I should take you up on your offer. I'm ready to go man. Where should I drive to?

Name a place anywhere on the continent (except

VOLKSWAGEN

Connecticut) and I'll be there in 48 hours, guaranteed. Just say the word, put me in one of your fine automobiles, and I'll go. I'll even transport stuff for you. Want a spark plug from Texas to Michigan? I'm your man. How about a lug nut from Vancouver to Saskabush? No Problem.

So when can I start? Do I have to go someplace exotic to register or can we do it online?

What kind of car will you give me? Can I just pick one up at a lot here in town and go? Can they leave the keys under the seat if I arrive after hours? And how does the pay work?

If I am driving all over the place, how do you get my paycheque to me? Should I bring a tent and foamy or will you give me a hotel allowance? If so, is it cash?

I am very excited about joining the V-Dub Team. Its almost as exciting as my first driving job. (which is why I can't go to Connecticut)

Should I bring a tent and foamy or will you give me a hotel allowance?

I am sure you will find me to be an exemplary citizen if you should check. (Again, Connecticut never proved anything, but don't bother checking there. I had a little personal disagreement with them so there may be some bias opinions in that state.)

So now you can stop that expensive ad campaign looking for drivers. I can do it, and I will proudly tell everyone I see that we are the best. I will go and get my car just as soon as you give

2

VOLKSWAGEN

me the OK in writing. (There will not be any mix up
this time because I'm not making assumptions about
stuff like that anymore, I've learned my lesson.)

I hope to hear from you soon as I need to travel
again, and I look forward to proudly wearing your
team clothing.

You will find that my attitude towards being on a
team is very healthy as I was raised with that old
maxim; There is no "I" in team, but without "ME",
all you've got is "T & A".

Glad to be onboard.
Jackson Snead

PS. I know a little trick to save on gas expenses
which could save a lot of money for the team.

VOLKSWAGEN

REPLY

From: Volkswagen
To: Jackson Snead
Sent: Monday, August 4, 2003
Subject: Driver Wanted, Driver Found

Dear Jackson,

Thank you for you interest in Volkswagen and being part of the team.

We apologize, but the "Driver's Wanted" is our marketing campaign targeted to bring in and continue to keep owners loyal to the Volkswagen family. Although, we do appreciate owners like you who are so enthusiastic about the company and so proud to be a part of the Volkswagen family.

You may forward your resume to our Human Resources Department at:

Volkswagen of America
3800 Hamlin Road
Auburn Hills, MI 48326
Attention: Human Resources

You may also check into Career Opportunities by clicking on VW the company and select Jobs @ VW. You can always send a resume that way, if you prefer.

We hope to hear from you soon and wish you luck in your future endeavors, wherever they may take you. Thank you for the great stories!

Brandy

Volktalk

COVER GIRL COSMETICS

COVER GUY

From: Jackson Snead
To: Cover Girl Cosmetics
Sent: Monday, August 15, 2005
Subject: Cover Guy

Dear Cover Girls,

The other day I heard Queen Latifah pitching your lipstick on TV saying how you could "send your lips to paradise". It kind of worked on me over a few days and I found myself wondering what that might feel like. So the other day, I broke down and got my wife's lipstick and smeared it on my lips. You guys were not kidding, it feels great. I had no idea that women were feeling this on their face when they put on make-up. No wonder they spend so much time primping.

...do you make lipstick in a man-size stick?

Your Fabulous Fuchsia felt so good that I started putting it on other parts of my face. I put it on my eyelids, cheeks and Adams apple. I was in ecstasy. I must have lay on the carpet for hours till my wife arrived home and began crying. I think she thought I had fallen down the stairs again. Turns out that she was upset that I had discovered her secret. Now she has to share her lipstick with me.

Since I'm not going to go and buy women's make-up for myself, she is complaining about me using so

5

COVER GIRL COSMETICS

much of hers.
My question to
you is, do you
make lipstick
in a man-size
stick, like maybe
the size of
bratwurst? Also,
are you thinking
of putting
out a line of
makeup for men
anytime soon? I
would buy it if
it was called
something like
Road-Kill Rouge
or Car-Crash
Crimson, you
know, something
manly. What about
isolating the

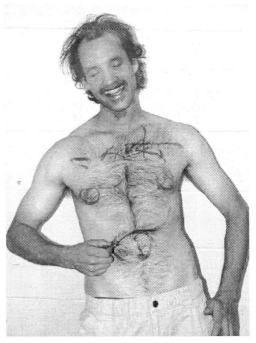

Better than crack!

paradise inducing elements of the make-up? You
could turn that into a body cream. With any luck
it would be addictive. I have a lab downstairs and
would do a few experiments for you if you wanted.

Please get back to me soon, as my wife is down to
the nubbins on her Pick-Me-Up-Pink again.

Thanks,
Jackson Snead

COVER GIRL COSMETICS

REPLY

From: Cover Girl Cosmetics
To: Jackson Snead
Sent Wednesday, August 17, 2005
Subject: Cover Guy

Dear Jackson

Thanks for the great message! I'm glad to hear how pleased you are with Cover Girl lip stick.. I'm sharing your comments with the rest of the team; I'm sure they'll be delighted. We appreciate your stopping by to let us know. As for Cover Girl for men, unfortunately we do not have a line for men in our cover girl products. You might want to visit the "Share Your Thoughts" section on our Global corporate website. This is a website specifically designed for those interested in sharing a quick thought or joining a feedback discussion for some of the products we make. Just go to http://www.pg.com and click on "Get in Touch with Us" and then on "Share Your Thoughts," where you'll see the list of brands that are currently involved in product sessions. Hope you'll check it out!

If you're interested in submitting a patented idea for review, just select "Submit a Patented Idea" from the "Share Your Thoughts" website. We're sorry but we can't accept any ideas in the areas of artwork, advertising, marketing, premiums, sales promotions, or product names.

I hope this helps. Stop by again soon.

Ann
Cover Girl Team

COVER GIRL COSMETICS

REPLY

From: Jackson Snead
To: Cover Girl Cosmetics
Sent: Monday, August 22, 2005
Subject: Hockey Highlights For Men

Dear Ann,

Since I last wrote to you, several things have developed. I started working on masculine makeup, and I am getting a great response. I have negotiated 3 real estate deals wearing "War Paint" as I call it. I get a much better deal than you might expect. I would try to describe some of my patterns to you, but it would be kind of like trying to describe a masterpiece by Rembrandt or Van Gogh.

Here is the situation, my idea for **Hockey Highlights For Men** make-up is taking off like gangbusters and I have several PeeWee league teams who intend to use it this year. They are very excited about the possibility of having colorful and intimidating faces to confront their opponents. The punk kids love it. How often does a product integrate punks into sports? I also have an NHL team interested in promoting and wearing designs for their home opener. We have several designs in creation now, and they will use a lot of makeup. This could be very good for you guys. We are going to need bright oranges, reds, blacks, and whites, as well as a collection of blue and mauves for the **Negotiators Collection**. Is it possible to get makeup made that will not run with sweat? How about smear proof?

8

COVER GIRL COSMETICS

We did have a concern from one of the coaches that the makeup will leave smears on the boards and the ice if the players get their faces slid along those surfaces. How about easy clean up makeup? Can you make up some packages for me to market special colors of my choosing? How about special labels?

Please get back to me soon, the season starts soon.

Jackson

REPLY

From: Cover Girl Cosmetics
To: Jackson Snead
Sent: Friday, August 26, 2005
Subject: Hockey Highlights For Men

Hi Jackson,

Thanks for contacting us again. We appreciate your interest in our Cover Girl products. You might want to visit the "Share Your Thoughts" section on our Global corporate website. This is a website specifically designed for those interested in sharing a quick thought or joining a feedback discussion for some of the products we make.

Just go to http://www.pg.com and click on "Get in Touch with Us" and then on "Share Your Thoughts," where you'll see the list of brands that are currently involved in product sessions. Hope you'll check it out! If you're interested in submitting a patented idea for review, just select "Submit a Patented Idea" from the "Share Your Thoughts" website. We're sorry but we can't accept any ideas in the areas of artwork, advertising, marketing, premiums, sales promotions, or product names.

I hope this helps. Stop by again soon.
Sincerely,
Duane   P&G Team

9

CALGARY FLAMES

HOCKEY HIGHLIGHTS FOR MEN

From: Jackson Snead
To: Calgary Flames
Sent: Monday August 29, 2005
Subject: Hockey Highlights For Men™

Dear Calgary Flames,

I represent an innovative line of
makeup called Hockey Highlights
For Men[a]. We are presently getting
ready for our launch and would like
to align with an NHL team to help
promote the product.

The makeup is based on the Maori
tradition of face tattoos and First
Nation's war paint. The concept is
to create a fierce competitive spirit
among young hockey players, which we think will
enhance the game by adding color and excitement.
Our studies have also shown increased camaraderie
among players with similar patterns. The makeup is
applied to player's faces in designs conducive to
the team's unique profile. In your case, it is easy
to imagine the players with flames painted on their
faces. Imagine when the Calgary Flames play the
Tampa Bay Lightning!!!

Wowee Zoweee!!!!!
What excitement for the crowd!!!

Players can customize their patterns depending on
their facial structure and these patterns will
then become identified with an individual player
or perhaps a line of players. That means a whole

10

CALGARY FLAMES

new edition of bubble-gum cards. It also leaves the door open for a product line of player face patterns to be marketed with our product. (For which your organization will share in the profit of course.) The concept is not limited to game night either. Our product has a whole range of day after products to highlight the injuries and bruises that are created by a rough game, (mostly blues and dark shades of mauve). We intend to market that part of the product to executives who negotiate for a living. Are you going to mess with someone who has a face like a purple eggplant? It kind of puts it right out there that this guy is not going to give up without a tough fight. It could give you that psychological edge needed to close a billion dollar deal. We hope to enlist the endorsements of several NHL tough guys for that part of our marketing plan. (Tiger Williams may be involved.)

Are you going to mess with someone who has a face like a purple eggplant?

We expect that a joint venture between our businesses will revolutionize and change the face of hockey. (Pun intended) We also expect that as pioneers, we (your organization included) will capture the lion's share of the multi-billion dollar men's make-up market. Please get back to me soon as the Flames are our first choice and we would like to catch the beginning of the season. We have several patterns ready for your team and can send things immediately.

Wait till you see the Pittsburgh Penguins!

Sincerely,
Jackson Snead

CALGARY FLAMES

REPLY

From: Calgary Flames Customer Service
To: Jackson Snead
Sent: Monday, August 29, 2005
Subject: RE: Hockey Highlights For Men

Thanks for your email and your interest in the Calgary Flames. Your email has been past along to our Hockey and Marketing departments for their review and consideration. If they are interested in your company and idea they will be in contact with you. All the best.

Go Flames Go!!!

Customer Service
Calgary Flames Hockey Club
(403)555-4646

Sign-up for the Flames newsletter today! Click here for more details: https://www.calgaryflames-secure.com/insider/

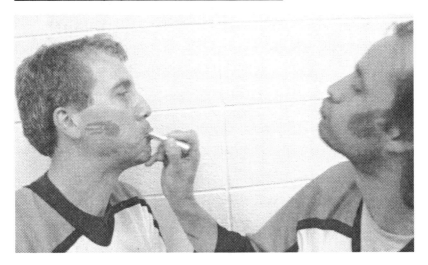

The right shade of lipstick can really improve a team's aggressiveness.

SAFEWAY STORES

BAGLESS BOB

From: Jackson Snead
To: Safeway Stores
Sent: Saturday, March 19, 2005
Subject: Bagless Bob

Dear Safeway,

I am writing on behalf of my friend Bagless Bob Bosun, who over the years has been treated quite fairly by your company. That is, until last Thursday.

Bagless Bob was pushing all his belongings through his favorite residential area when he was approached by a Policeman claiming to be acting on your behalf. After several minutes of verbal exchanges and aerobic activity, Bob was forced to give up all his worldly possessions to the police officer. The officer claimed to be taking the shopping cart back to Safeway as he suspected that Bob had illegally obtained it.

Bob insisted that he had paid for it but could not provide a receipt and so he lost his belongings. (Included was a vintage copy of The Times-Colonist and a priceless collection of bottlecaps.)

...he was able to identify his cart by the wobbly wheel and teeth marks on the push bar.

Upon returning to the store, he was able to identify his cart by the wobbly wheel and teeth marks on the push bar, but the store's assistant

13

SAFEWAY STORES

manger would not release his property to him and simply put it back in the line with the other carts. Luckily, Bob was able to purchase it again after cleaning several windshields and was able to continue on his way.

Unfortunately, all of his belongings were lost and so he is now pushing an empty cart around town until he finds appropriate replacements. This brings me to the point of my letter, Bob has asked me to write to you for a receipt so that the next time he is stopped by the police he can prove that he owns the cart. He paid one dollar cash and the cart it was attached to had no means to issue a receipt. Obviously, if Bob has the cart, he paid for it as they are not released from their rack without payment. If he did not pay for it, it could have been a gift but that is not illegal either.

Bob is quite pleased by your pricing structure and has been a loyal customer for many years. He

Sometimes, Bob just has to scratch.

SAFEWAY STORES

always chooses Safeway for his vehicles. (Canadian
Superstore charges $2 for their carts) Bob would
hate to have to switch allegiance after owning the
Cadillac of carts for so many years.

Keep in mind that he does provide a valuable
service for you as he proudly displays the
Safeway logo walking through the more exclusive
neighborhoods on the way to the park where he
sleeps.

I am sure upon fair consideration of this matter
you will reply favorably. Your acceptance by e-mail
should suffice as a receipt.

Thank You,
Jackson Snead

REPLY

From: Safeway
To: Jackson Snead
Sent: Monday, March 21, 2005
Subject: Bagless Bob

Dear Mr. Snead:

Thank you for your recent correspondence regarding your friend and
the Safeway shopping cart. Unfortunately Safeway does not sell it's
carts to the general public or piecemeal, so I would have to say that
your friend Bob has been tricked. Only our corporate office would
allow the sale of a cart, and they are not going to send a receipt
to your friend. We apologize for any inconvenience this may have
caused you.

If you would like to discuss this further, please reply to this email or
call our toll free number at 1-800-555-3929 and reference contact

SAFEWAY STORES

I.D. 7413147. One of our associates will be happy to assist you.

We appreciate your business and look forward to seeing you soon. Thank you for shopping at Safeway.

Sincerely,

Mark Allen
Customer Service Representative

REPLY

From: Jackson Snead
To: Safeway
Sent: Tuesday, March 22, 2005
Subject: Bagless Bob

Dear Mark,

I think you are right. Bagless Bob was tricked. I read Bob your reply and upon further discussion, it turns out that the policeman was not wearing a uniform, did not produce a badge or offer any sort of identification. So I think you are right, Bob has been tricked out of all his worldly possessions. (again)

Although he was quite sure to have identified his cart, Bob does not really have the forensic experience to distinguish between bite marks on shopping cart handles and he could have been mistaken. Bob now thinks it was really the bottlecap collection they were after and that the cart is probably in some woodland stream-bed stopping large chunks of water-plants in its grill. It's a good thing he kept the most valuable caps in his shoe.

SAFEWAY STORES

Anyway, we are glad that Safeway had no hand in it
and are thankful that you are willing to give him
another cart without purchase. We do understand
that your corporate office would not want to issue
a receipt for a measly $1.00 and that Bob will
just have to suck it up and be a man the next time
someone tries to rip him off. (I told him to take
Karate, but no go.) Bob extends his heartfelt
thanks and is comforted by your insight into this
matter. To show his appreciation, Bob has written,
(or is writing) a song to honor the occasion. He
says he will sing it all day long to anyone who
will listen. We hope it can become like a Safeway
anthem. Most of it is pretty good. You might want
to use it in a commercial. Bob wants to know who he
should send it to.

Thanks
Jackson Snead

REPLY

From: Safeway
To: Jackson Snead
Sent: Tuesday, March 22, 2005
Subject: Bagless Bob

Dear Mr. Snead:

I have received your reply email and would like to take the time to
respond. Bob can go to our web site and under "Our Company" click
the suppliers link. It will lead to the area were people who wish to be
vendors of service providers fill out a form and send it to our head
office.

Mark Allen
Customer Service Representative

SAFEWAY STORES

REPLY

Dear Mark

Here is the song which I discussed with you last week that Bagless Bob wrote. We think it is really quite good. You may already know the tune as it is quite intuitive. I had no trouble picking it up, and I'm tone deaf. See what you think, Bob says he's got a million of them. He is just asking for some coupons at the deli counter if you decide to use it. Here we go....

I'd like to buy the world a home and furnish it with love, from Safeway
Grow apple trees and honey bees, and snow white turtle doves, from Safeway
I'd like to teach the world to sing in perfect harmony, at Safeway
I'd like to buy the world a Coke and keep it company, in Safeway
[Repeat the last two lines, and in the background:]
It's the real thing, Coke is what the world wants today, from Safeway.

Kind of makes you feel good doesn't it? Let us know.

Jackson Snead

GREYHOUND BUS LINES

A TICKET TO RIDE

From: Jackson Snead
To: Greyhound Bus Lines
Sent: Tuesday, August 23, 2005
Subject: A Ticket To Ride

Dear Greyhound,

After 65 years of sailing the seven seas, I have decided that my seafaring days are over. Now I am starting to road-surf the seven continents. I have decided to book steerage class on board one of your fine bus vessels to cruise North America.

I will be shoving off from Victoria this fall, intend to crest the Rocky Mountains and cruise through the gentle rolling swells of Alberta and the flat grasslands of the prairies.

My first destination is to be Beaverton, Ontario, where I am obligated to settle a debt. Which brings me to my reason for writing. For years, I have been hampered by a disability to recognize danger and have relied upon others and special service animals to alert me when required. I used to travel with Polly, my African gray parrot, who dutifully alerted me to danger from her perch upon my shoulder. Several times I was able to dodge a cannon ball due to her keen instincts and survival skills. Sadly, Polly was lost at sea after she pecked me in the eye one to many times.

Then, while getting the eye patch during shore leave, I was able to acquire Corrigan, an alarm beaver. He has served me well for many years, and I

GREYHOUND BUS LINES

owe him a great debt for saving my life many times over. Once, while sailing on the Spanish Main, his determination to alert me to danger caused him to gnaw completely through my wooden leg, making me list to starboard just enough to counter-act the rum and keep me from falling over the side and being lost at sea.

Another time, while searching for the lost city of Eldorado, he drove off a crocodile with a swift whack of his tail while I was stuck by my hand-hook to a vine.

Now, after years of devoted service, Corrigan is retiring to Beaverton, where he shall live the rest of his life recanting swashbuckling tales of bravery to the other beavers. As a result, I will need two tickets to Beaverton, Ontario, departing in mid September. I have a few questions though, as your land-sailor ways are still mysterious to me.

1) Do I have to pay full price for Corrigan's ticket? He only weighs 38 lbs.

2) Can you tell me how long the trip takes? I need to pack enough diapers for him. It's not as if we can just hose off the deck anymore.

3) Can we take a couple of extra long breaks during the voyage so that Corrigan can have a good chew on the local trees?

He's getting to be an old man too, and he takes a while to eat, especially since he got those new scrimshaw dentures.

Captain Jackson Snead

GREYHOUND BUS LINES

REPLY

From: Greyhound Bus Lines
To: Jackson Snead
Sent: Wednesday, August 24, 2005
Subject: Re: A Ticket To Ride

1) Sorry but Greyhound Canada does not accept pets for transportation - 2) Victoria - Vancouver - is serviced by Pacific Coach Lines - 1-800-661-1725 - 3) Greyhound Canada does not service Beaverton/On - the closest location is Orillia /Barrie or Toronto - 4) Please see attachment for information on Canada Travel Pass - 5) If you travel straight through , the trip from Victoria - Barrie is about 75 hrs.

Thank you for visiting our website.
If you need additional fare and schedule information,
please call 1-800-661-8747 or 403-265-9111.

All fares and schedules are subject to change without notice.

All fares are in Canadian funds including applicable taxes unless otherwise noted.

BJ, Greyhound Canada PSC

Two tickets to Beaverton, please.

LONDON SCHOOL OF BUSINESS

SWIMMING WITH SHARKS

From: Jackson Snead
To: London School Of Business
Sent: Saturday, October 29, 2005
Subject: Swimming With Sharks

Dear Sirs

I give a business course, "Swimming With Sharks", which is extremely relevant and timely for our current business climate. It has a very high satisfaction rate among the companies that send their employee's to it.

Swimming With Sharks is designed to motivate and challenge managers and employees to think outside the box and come up with creative survival tactics. Many employers send their employees to the course to test their dedication and loyalty while others put their job candidates through the course as a screening process.

The great thing about the course is that the results are immediately apparent and most students have epiphanies during our course.

Many graduates go on to achieve greatness while we never hear again from the ones who fail.

For the last 3 years, I have been teaching the course at Nigeria Business and Cooking College in Lagos and have many rave reviews from local upper level personnel.

In the past, the course was given in the open ocean, but I recently acquired a 15,000-gallon portable aquarium which can be set up on campus.

LONDON SCHOOL OF BUSINESS

It even has viewing windows for the underwater observation of the participants. I have a collection of seventeen sharks, including an eleven-foot hammerhead, (always a crowd pleaser) and four medium sized great white sharks. (There used to be twenty sharks, but the summer break changed the feeding dynamics.)

I am currently setting up my summer semester schedule. It is a three-day course and requires 7 days set up and teardown. I only have three spaces available.

Please let me know if you would like to schedule this course.

Jackson Snead

REPLY

From: London School of Business
To: Jackson Snead
Sent: Monday, October 31, 2005
Subject: Re: Swimming With Sharks

Thank you for your email.

Unfortunately your course is not something that we would be interested in.

Kind regards

Ms. Minnow
Communications

STARBUCKS

SPECIAL COFFEE

From: Jackson Snead
To: Starbucks
Sent: Monday, January 26, 2004
Subject: Special Coffee

Dear Starfolks,

I am a loyal customer and probably will be for many years to come. I'm the kind of person you want to have enjoying your product. When I go out for coffee, I don't call it coffee any more. I call it Starbucks. When I suggest to a friend that we go for a refreshing hot beverage, I say "Lets go to Starbucks" and they always say Yes, because I pay.

I did the math, and over the years, I have spent over $150,000.00 on your coffee alone. Lots more if I count the cups and muffins. I wonder what the record is? Anyway, I am writing to you to get the answers to two questions.

1) The other day I heard about some coffee-beans that had been ingested by a tiger before they were roasted and made into a brew. Apparently the taste was incredible. I would sure like to try some of that. Are you guys doing it? I would buy it. I'll bet it picks up some kind of special tiger energy as it passes through the tiger and it becomes real powerful and tasty.

I have spent over $150,000.00 on your coffee alone.

You could come up with a slogan like "It puts a

24

STARBUCKS

tiger in your tank". People would remember that slogan because of the Esso thing, it would catch on for sure. Maybe you could keep a real tiger in some of your larger stores and they could be the onsite processing units.

I think people would sit around for hours if they knew that the tiger was actually processing and energizing their cup of coffee. Imagine, actually watching a tiger prepare your coffee.

I also heard that the tiger's habitat was disappearing, so there's probably lots of tigers that need a place to live. With all the stores that you guys have, you could give all of them new homes. It could be promoted as environmentally friendly since you are helping the tigers. How cool would Starbucks be then?

Imagine, actually watching a tiger prepare your coffee.

So please tell me if you are going to do that, because I'd like to be in the loop and get ready for it. My next question is: Why, if you have a double glass entrance doors to your stores, do you keep one side of them open, and the other side locked? Do you have a set pattern? Is it right side open going in, and left side open going out? Or Vice-Versa.

I swear they changed it on me while I was in the store the other day.

I came speeding out through the right side entrance door and it didn't move. You might have heard about this at your office already, because everyone in the place had a good laugh. I would have too, if

25

STARBUCKS

I hadn't been so concerned about the pain and my muffin getting wet.(It did and it fell apart).

So anyway, I would sure like to know if there is a standard unlocking procedure because I visit so many of your stores and I would like to develop a standard entrance and exit procedure.

Maybe you could put a sticker on the glass entrance door that is locked, kind of like stickers on your windows at home that are shaped like birds so that sparrows don't fly into the glass.

Maybe the sticker could have your new tiger slogan on it. Please get back to me quickly. I'll be able to hold a cup again soon, and I want to go get a Starbucks without fear of the doors.

Thanks
Jackson Snead

REPLY

From: Starbucks
To: Jackson Snead
Sent: Wednesday, January 28, 2004
Subject: Re: Special Coffee

Dear Mr. Snead:

Thank you for contacting Starbucks Coffee Company.

Unfortunately, we don't carry the type of coffee you are referring too. As for the doors, I would ask the store manager as to why one side remains locked.

Thank you again for contacting Starbucks.

STARBUCKS

If you have any further questions or concerns, please contact us at info@starbucks.com or call (800) 23-LATTE to speak with a customer relations representative.

Sincerely,

Allisen
Customer Relations

REPLY

From: Jackson Snead
To: Starbucks
Sent: Saturday, February 7, 2004
Subject: Kopi Luwak Coffee

Dear Allisen,

A while back I asked about a specialty coffee which I thought had been passed through a tiger. I'm very embarrassed to find out that I was completely wrong about that.

In retrospect, it makes no sense at all and I apologize for any inconvenience that I may have caused while you had to research my request. It was totally foolish to think that a tiger would excrete beans suitable for your

It was totally foolish to think that a tiger would excrete beans suitable for your fine stores

fine stores. And of course it was totally foolish to think that an animal as big as a tiger could be kept in each of your stores. (Although I'm sure it would attract more customers, not that you need that.)

27

STARBUCKS

So the day of revelation came just before Christmas when I spotted the attached article involving Kopi Luwak coffee. This is made by the native Indonesian feral cat, a luwak, or palm civet as it is known locally.

Apparently this is quite an exotic tasting flavor and you can find lots of info on the web regarding this coffee if you do a Google search for Kopi Luwak.

This kind of puts things into perspective. I think it would be a lot easier to keep luwaks in your stores than tigers. When I think of the liability that you would be exposed to should a tiger get loose, (especially one that has been eating coffee beans) it could have ruined you.

On the other hand, if a luwak gets loose, it would just be like an ordinary cat getting out.

It would probably come back too, as do people to your stores, owing to their addiction to coffee. Where else is a cat going to get coffee?

So I think I've got most of the bugs worked out now, and I have a definite plan to import a few luwaks and see how we do at coffee processing.

Since you are my favorite store, I thought I would give you guys first crack at the opportunity to work with me on this project.

There are probably a few things I have missed and that can only be discovered by experience, but I've had cats before, and I still have the litter boxes etc..

STARBUCKS

I'm sure this will be a great success and all
we need is a new marketing slogan. I have ruled
out "Cat's Ass Coffee" because it's already
copyrighted, but I'm sure something will come up
that suits the product.

How about it?

Jackson Snead

TIMES

'Fermented' coffee safe

GUELPH, Ont. (CP) — Kopi Luwak coffee — the $1,300 a kilogram delicacy collected from the backside of an Indonesian feral cat called the luwak — is safe, says Massimo Marcone, a University of Guelph food scientist.

Macone found Kopi Luwak coffee has lower bacterial counts than regular coffee.

"As a food scientist, I'm skeptical that anything being in contact with feces is safe," he says. "But tests revealed that the Kopi Luwak beans had negligible amounts of enteric (pathogenic) organisms.

The low bacteria count is likely due to the washing process performed by Indonesians collecting the beans, he says. The "cherry" or endocarp surrounding the bean is not completely digested by the luwak; it must be removed during processing. This probably leads to a more thorough washing process, he says.

Known as the palm civet in its native country, the luwak feeds on coffee beans. Its stomach acids and enzymes digest the beans' cherry-like covering and ferment the beans themselves, before they are excreted. It's believed that fermentation process gives the coffee a unique flavour.

29

STARBUCKS

REPLY

From: Starbucks
To: Jackson Snead
Sent: Monday, February 9, 2004
Subject: RE: Kopi Luwak Coffee

Dear Mr. Snead:

Thank you for contacting Starbucks Coffee Company.

We have heard about the coffee that is passed through a monkey (this is what I thought you were referring to in your previous email). This is some interesting news.

Thanks for thinking of us and devising a plan to introduce this coffee to Starbucks! Thank you again for contacting Starbucks.

If you have any further questions or concerns, please contact us at info@starbucks.com or call (800) 23-LATTE to speak with a customer relations representative.

Sincerely,

Allisen
Customer Relations

REPLY

From: Jackson Snead
To: Starbucks
Sent: Monday, March 8, 2004
Subject: Making Some Coffee For You

Dear Allisen

It's been a while, but as promised, I am getting

30

STARBUCKS

back to you with a golden opportunity. A little while ago, I got the luwaks as planned, and now I have some of that Kopi Luwak Coffee almost ready to go. The first batch should come out tomorrow. I had a couple of false starts because I misunderstood some of the technical terminology.

Apparently, when speaking of cherries, (and only when speaking of coffee), it refers to the bean as it grows on the tree in its raw form. Oh, that quirky English language.

So now this is the voice of experience talking, cherry pits will not under any circumstances be suitable to brew a beverage with, and especially after a luwak has "had it's way with it".

So I am now the proud owner of Ginger and Wanda, a grand pair of luwaks that will be the parents of my herd. I had never seen a luwak before I purchased them, but it is obvious that they are related to domestic cats. And who knew there was a luwak dealer at the trailer park?

In fact, as long as they can poop, they're OK in my books.

He got them in within half an hour of my request. He said he got them out of a shipment destined for New York, but because of my willingness to out bid the other buyers, I was successful in obtaining the animals.

He said there will not be any more in for years, and that I had successfully stymied my competition. So it was a wise investment. J.D., (the dealer) also told me that they are both pregnant so I can expect 13-14 kittens in a couple of months.

STARBUCKS

Its unlikely that Ginger and Wanda have the same
mate, as they lived on opposite sides of the
country when wild, so I figure there will be enough
genetic diversity to create a well rounded herd
from those two and their kittens.

But you know, its not like I am raising them to be
rocket scientists or anything. In fact, as long as
they can poop, they're OK in my books.

Anyway, like I said, I had a couple of false
starts, but now I figure I am ready to start the
production. It will be limited for a few more
months, until the kittens are born & weaned, but I
have a unique marketing plan, which you may want to
adapt should we enter into a business agreement.
That is: to sell the days production the day before
it is produced.

The customer actually reserves their morning cup
of coffee. Here's how that works. The luwaks eat
the cherries (now remember, coffee in the raw form,
not Okanogan fruit) in the evening, then in the
morning, I pick it up somewhere in the living room
and clean it up and send it out to the buyer via
courier. They can roast it and grind it themselves,
it's part of the total experience that we sell.

Plus it sets us apart from the competition. Each
buyer gets enough for one cuppa-joe. This way, I
sell all production before manufacturing and the
price doesn't seem so much per pound.

Owing to the rarity of the product, and high
production costs, I have to charge $435.00 per cup.
So not too many people are going to pay for more
then one or two cups at a time. I guess I'll know
better after a week or so when I've gone through a

STARBUCKS

Wanda hacks up a latte...

STARBUCKS

week of production and sales.

Because, as I am sure you know, with even the most well prepared plans, there can be unforeseen difficulties. I have sold out my first days run to my wife's cousin from Spain, Jose. I guess if he likes it, he is going to distribute it through the Spanish Conquistadors (I think that is some sort of service organization that he belongs to. They seem to work closely with the police in their community.)

So I am just writing to offer you a few days worth of production, since you guys are in the biz too, and I thought you would like the opportunity to book early. I'll give you a discount if you clean your own beans.

I'm thinking "Eight Lives Coffee", what do you think?

Jackson Snead

REPLY

From: Starbucks
To: Jackson Snead
Sent: Thursday, March 11, 2004
Subject: RE: Making Some Coffee For You

Dear Mr. Snead:

Thank you for contacting Starbucks Coffee Company. I appreciate the detailed information you sent regarding the services your company provides.

Starbucks is very satisfied with the results from current vendors, but

STARBUCKS

as we continue to grow our needs might change. With this in mind, please send a proposal describing your product/service to:

Starbucks Coffee Company R-UI1
PO Box 34067
Seattle, WA 98124-1067

**Please do not send samples.

Thank you again for contacting Starbucks Coffee Company. I hope you continue to enjoy Starbucks Coffee for years to come.

Sincerely,
Michael
customer relations representative

REPLY

From: Jackson Snead
To: Starbucks
Sent: Monday, March 15, 2004
Subject: Whoops

Dear Michael,

I've got to tell you, I didn't expect this. You know that old Murphy slaw,when everything gets all mixed up together and goes crazy?

It turns out that when a luwak eats coffee cherries, they go absolutely nuts.

In retrospect, I should have kept them in cages, but they seemed so gentle and playful. Who would have thought that under that short patchy fur, there could come a viciousness unleashed like the flaming, thrashing, slashing, hell fury that tears at the fabric of human sanity. They seemed to

35

STARBUCKS

have had a reaction to me feeding them the coffee cherries.

Anyway, when I got back from the emergency room, Ginger and Wanda were long gone.

I guess if the sound of my screams and the sirens didn't drive them completely out of the neighborhood, the sound of my exploding Boler trailer would have pretty much sealed the deal. Now, I have no herd, I am stuck having to pay back Jose for his coffee, and I owe JD (the dealer) $340.000.00 from the bidding war for Ginger and Wanda. (Did you ever get caught up in a bidding war for something? Man, you have got to be careful.)

They seemed to have had a reaction to me feeding them the coffee cherries

I doubt if I'll qualify for any kind of farm disaster relief, but I'll try. JD gave me till Thursday though, which was generous, and a date upon which we could both agree.

So I have put up posters with Ginger and Wanda's picture on it, and I have got quite a few responses, but it's never them. Just another kitty with a back alley haircut and some kid trying to collect a $1000.00 reward.

The problem is though, after I reject them, they still leave the cat. I've got about 29 shaved cats hanging about my yard, counting the Nair twins.

Needless to say, I won't be sending coffee your direction soon. I think I might have to come up with another plan.

36

STARBUCKS

Oh yeah, I still have a boxcar load of coffee cherries. Do you guys want them? They're still in the boxcar.

Please let me know soon because I don't want them to spoil.

Maybe it's Seven Lives Coffee now.

Jackson Snead

LEE VALLEY TOOLS

DUCT TAPE

From: Jackson Snead
To: Lee Valley Tools
Sent: Thursday, November 07, 2002
Subject: Duct tape

Dear Sirs,

My wife and I have been very satisfied Lee Valley customers over the years, and it looks like that is going to continue.

I was looking through your catalogue this morning in preparation for my trip to Africa and I came upon the perfect item. On page 33 of the Christmas 2002 catalog, item 25U05.01, The original Duct tape. This is just what I need.

I am a great believer in bring-em-back-alive and was wondering how I was going to bring back the animals that I want. Then I saw in your ad that this duct tape can be used to restrain a bull elephant and my problem was solved.

Now I can trap the elephant and restrain him for shipping. What a great idea! I had no idea that duct tape could be used in this way. I was all prepared to get a huge cage to ship him back, but now I find all that redundant. Before I order though, I do have some questions about it's

LEE VALLEY TOOLS

application. I don't want to buy too little, or be disappointed like I was with my little "Sea Monkey" experiment. (Most monkeys can't swim at all and they would rather be in trees.)

1) How many rolls do you think I will need? (I expect to get a big elephant) Will one roll do, or should I get a couple just to be sure?

2) Do you have any diagrams as to how to restrain a bull elephant? Should I tape all four legs together or do the front and back ones separately?

3) What do I do with the trunk and tail? Can I tape the trunk to the tail to keep them from flailing around, or should I just tape them to a leg?

4) Should the ears be taped back to prevent flopping, or are they OK? I don't think the ears have any bones to break.

5) Will this tape work for antelope too, and is there any way to easily remove the hair from the tape?

6) Do you think I could construct a trap with this tape as well? Maybe using the sticky side like a spider web, or do you think the elephant will notice it and not fall for that?

LEE VALLEY TOOLS

Please get back to me soon, as I leave for Africa
shortly and want to order the duct tape so that it
gets to me well in advance of my departure date.

Thanks so much for solving my dilemma,

Jackson Snead

REPLY

From: Lee Valley Tools
To: Jackson Snead
Sent: Tuesday, November 12, 2002
Subject: RE: Duct Tape

Mr Snead,
We have received your email, and are delighted that you have read
our copy so diligently, and intend to follow our recommendations
scrupulously....

Please see our answers to your questions, interspersed with your
text below....

1) How many rolls do you think I will need? (I expect to
get a big elephant) Will one roll do, or should I get a
couple just to be sure?

The answer here is not as obvious as one would
suspect. Much like the case with clamps (you always
need one or two more than you have), you can never
have too much duct tape. How much you should
purchase is really a function of contingency
planning.

The less "extra" equipment you have with
you, the more duct tape you'll probably
need. In addition, significant user

frustration can be avoided by having at least 1 roll per person actively involved in pachyderm restraining.

2) Do you have any diagrams as to how to restrain a bull elephant? Should I tape all four legs together or do the front and back ones separately?

Alas, we have discontinued the pachyderm restraint plans (actual size), as we had to fold then 72 times to fit within postal size limits.

While we were happy to do this, several customers reported that the amount of time required to refold the plan was too time consuming, and most male users just never opened them...

As for the legs - will you be restraining trained, or untrained elephants? If the former, it's quite straightforward - just have it mount the standard #7 circus stool (the four foot stance) - and tape away. If untrained, front and back separately works best.

3) What do I do with the trunk and tail? Can I tape the trunk to the tail to keep them from flailing around, or should I just tape them to a leg?

Dealing with the trunk is a simple matter - please see our "trunk tie-down" on the following web page: http://www.leevalley.com/garden/page.asp?page=10135&category=2,43288,42182&a bspage=1&ccurrency=1&SID=

Restraint of the tail is deemed by most to be unnecessary, and could even result in an adverse accumulation, and subsequent catastrophic expulsion, of what used to be plant matter.

4) Should the ears be taped back to prevent flopping, or are they OK? I don't think the ears have any bones to break.

LEE VALLEY TOOLS

Freedom of ear movement is necessary for the animal to properly regulate body temperature...

5) Will this tape work for antelope too, and is there any way to easily remove the hair from the tape?

For really hairy animals, we'd suggest gaffers tape - which should totally avoid negative depilatory effects.It's not quite as strong, but then again - an antelope's no bull elephant....

6) Do you think I could construct a trap with this tape as well? Maybe using the sticky side like a spider web, or do you think the elephant will notice it and not fall for that?

We hesitate to recommend for or against applications we haven't personally tried... We will post this exchange in few woodworking forums to see if other users have suggestions...

Please get back to me soon, as I leave for Africa shortly and want to order the duct tape so that it gets to me well in advance of my departure date.

Not a problem. We'd also recommend that you review shipping requirements at: http://www1.iata.org/cargooperations/liveanimals/index

Thanks so much for solving my dilemma,

And thank you for your continued custom.

Cheers,

Rob Lee
Lee Valley Tools Ltd.

LEE VALLEY TOOLS

Thanks, Lee Valley!

43

LEE VALLEY TOOLS

From: Jackson Snead
To: Lee, Robin
Sent: Friday, November 15, 2002
Subject: Re: Duct Tape Answers

Dear Robin,

Thank you for your most informative e-mail and links. I am especially impressed with the depth of knowledge that you Lee Valley people exhibit. I thought you would think I was crazy.

Thanks for endorsing my expedition. I'll put a little sign on my Jeep that speaks kindly of Lee Valley. If you have any suggestions, I'm open to them. Maybe something like," Animal restraints by Lee Valley" I am considering my options at this point, and will probably end up using both gaffer and duct tape on my expedition.

Your animal shipping link was quite useful, and I have decided to take a ship. I am told I will have to purchase an entire row of seats if I chose to travel back with the elephant by air. I thought the courts recently decided that issue; One fare, one traveler.

Oh well, you can't fight the airlines. At least this way I can bring back more animals, and am adjusting my plans accordingly. I will probably want some of those extra large crocodile clips as well. Do they come in a larger size?

Currently learning Swahili,

Jackson Snead

44

LEE VALLEY TOOLS

REPLY

From: Lee Valley Tools
To: Jackson Snead
Sent: Tuesday, November 19, 2002
Subject: Duct Tape Answers

Mr Snead,

Ninyi haja ako dawa sasa ....(Swahili)

Thanks for the laugh...

Cheers,

Rob Lee

Extra large crocodile clips required.

WEEKLY WORLD NEWS

CARGO CULT GOD

From: Albert Swinehinderson
To: Weekly World News
Sent: Wednesday, April 30, 2003
Subject: Cargo Cult God

Dear Sirs,
Here is the text from an article in the South
Island Eye newspaper, a small paper that circulates
around the Pacific Islands. It is about a friend of
mine, Jackson Snead, who set out to sail around the
world and stopped halfway. I can put you in touch
with him if you like.

International Yachtsman becomes Island God

International yachtsman, Jackson Snead, has become the
god of Pomeratu, a small island in the South Pacific inhabited
by a cargo cult. Cargo cults are well known in this part of
the Pacific, and were formed when the American military
pulled out of their WW2 island bases and left millions of
dollars worth of supplies behind for the locals to have.
The tribe on Pomeratu worshipped Jack Frum, the American
G.I. who said he would bring them more stuff one day. (All
they know about Jack Frum is that he was Jack from America.)
The belief then formed that in order to obtain more goods, the
natives had to attract more of the cargo planes, and Jack Frum
would return bringing everything. As a result, the natives built
primitive airports complete with control towers made from
sticks and jungle vines. The island culture had no exposure to
the outside world before the war, and very little since. They
developed bizarre rituals involving dancing, chanting, and

46

licking hallucinogenic snails to create visions of the great day. Then, while on a round the world trip, Jackson Snead was blown off course by a storm and took shelter in Pomeratu's small lagoon. When he introduced himself as Jackson, the cultists thought he said Jack's son, and believed their savior had finally arrived. A great celebration occurred that night and the next day the storm wrecked a Chinese Freighter.

Nearly 500 shipping containers washed up on Pomeratu containing everything from food, generators, TV's, and jewelry. The natives believe Jackson Snead was the cause of the windfall, and he isn't about to tell them any different. The natives worship Jackson now

The cultists thought he said Jack's son, and believed their savior had finally arrived.

and do what ever he asks. He has the best hut on the hill and plans to stay. "Paradise couldn't be so great," he says.

When a reporter asked one of the elder tribesmen whether he felt foolish believing in the cargo cult, he replied," We have been worshipping Jack Frum for only 50 years and we got TV's. You Christians have been worshipping for 2000 years and when was the last time Jesus gave you a TV?"

I hope you can use this,
Albert Swinehinderson

REPLY

To: Albert Swinehinderson
From: Kay @ Weekly World News
Sent: Monday, March 3, 2003
Subject: Tell Us More

Dear Albert

Thank you for your email regarding your friend who has become a living God. Is it possible for you to put me in touch with him, either by phone or email? This sounds like an interesting story

Kay

From: Jackson Snead
To: Kay @ Weekly World News
Sent: Friday, March 7, 2003
Subject: Anytime

Mahalo Kay

I got an e-mail earlier today that said you wanted to talk to me. I don't get to a phone often, but I do have a pretty good computer and satellite

uplink. Might have a phone in one of the other containers but we haven't found one yet. Still got a few to look through. Not really to motivated though, kind of like the way I'm living now. Be glad to fill you in on some of the details. Got

Sillius Snaillius Pomeratus

to go now, I think the party is about to start again. We've got a fresh bunch of snails for tonight. I love Pomeratu and Pomeratu loves me,

Jackson Snead

REPLY

From: Kay
To: Jackson Snead
Sent: Monday, March 17, 2003
Subject: RE: Anytime

Mr. Snead: I'm so sorry to have put off replying to you. I'm sending you some initial questions for the "interview." Also, do you have any photos you could e-mail to us? I think they'd need to be 300-dpi resolution or better. I'll have some more questions as we go along, but these should do for a start:

1. I'm attaching the original e-mail that we received, about the circumstances of your arrival on Pomeratu and how you became the island god. Is the account correct?

2. Where are you from originally, and how old are you?

3. What was your occupation before landing on Pomeratu?

4. Did you leave any family behind? If so, have you communicated with them? Do you miss them?

5. When and how did you wash up on Pomeratu?

6. How did the natives greet you at first? Were you in any danger, and if so were you scared at all?

7. What's Pomeratu like? Population, economy, climate. Is it pretty much like the tropical paradise that most of us think a South Pacific island is? It sounds like people don't work too hard but just relax and enjoy life. Well, I hope we can still do this despite my seeming to be ignoring you!

-- Kay

WEEKLY WORLD NEWS

REPLY

From: Jackson Snead
To: Kay @ Weekly World News
Sent: Tuesday, March 18, 2003
Subject: Life On Pomeratu

Dear Kay

Don't worry about ignoring me; I get plenty of attention as it is.

That newspaper account is pretty close, but I wasn't really on a round the world trip, I was actually drifting aimlessly in an amphibious Kenyan Army landing craft that I liberated to escape the wrath of M'bumbu M'bumba, a Kenyan warlord. He was a bit upset with me when his chicken future stocks failed to mature and his investment was eaten by a wedding reception party at Sunday brunch. Anyway, I don't advocate taking an amphibious craft without a compass out to sea and losing sight of land. The ocean is a surprisingly big place.

To give you my history, I am originally from Baklavania and was traded for a box of sausages when I was just a baby. My adoptive parents were the royal entertainers and specialized in animal acts. They were subsequently banished from the country after their camels went wild at the princess's sweet 16 party. They attempted to gain favor again by going to Manitoba and recruiting dancing polar bears. Unfortunately, polar bears would rather eat then dance and I was left behind as my guardians ran like the cowardly chicken chasers that they are. Luckily, I was then adopted by a maternal bear and lived with her for a couple of years till I was found by tourists in Churchill, Manitoba, when Bear-Ma was looking for take-out.

I do miss my family, Bear-Ma especially, she would make me the cutest little sealskin pullovers by flipping a seal inside out. I looked like a little pink traffic cone running around the tundra. Unfortunately, she didn't quite get that whole arm-hole thing and I spent hours rolling around in circles when I fell over. I am also curious about my real mother and why she loved those sausages so much and where would I get me some of those.

Luckily for me, Pomeratu is one of the last cargo cult islands in the South Pacific and I was washed up with 457 containers of consumer goods from a wrecked Chinese Freighter.

My original reason for going to Kenya was that I was looking for my birth mother. Somehow I got hooked into running a ponzi scheme in the stock market and as mentioned, ended up lost at sea. After many weeks of living off the fish that I would catch with a safety pin and shoelace, I encountered a typhoon and was barely alive when I washed up on the shores of Pomeratu.

Luckily for me, Pomeratu is one of the last cargo cult islands in the South Pacific and I was washed up with 457 containers of consumer goods from a wrecked Chinese Freighter. Faced with the choice of being or eating dinner, I took credit for bringing the cargo to the thankful natives and was immediately elevated to the status of living God.

WEEKLY WORLD NEWS

Presently, I rule supreme. I have them prepare my food, sing to me, dance for me, and even blanket toss me as I wish. It's a great life here. There are about 1000 people in an aboriginal type of civilization heavily influenced by the shaman. They have plenty of edible vegetation and a native species of snail that produces a psychotropic effect if you lick it. Pomeratu is a pretty idyllic place, a tropical volcanic island with flora and fauna to match. If it weren't for the circling albatross every 35 minutes being chased by the barking border collies, I would lose track of time completely.

Speaking of time, I hear the dogs and that means it's time for dancing again. Luckily, the Chinese were shipping beer right along side of those useless TV's. Let me know if you want more info.

Jackson.

Sometimes I just sit around in my underpants giggling to myself.

FLORSHEIM SHOES

WALKER TEXAS MOUSE KILLER

From: Jackson Snead
To: Florsheim Shoes
Subject: Walker Texas Mouse-killer
Sent: Tuesday, October 12, 2004

Dear Florsheim,

It has been a little over a week since I sent you my inquiry regarding my squeaky shoes. With a company like yours, I'm sure you don't get to many complaints or negative comments, and one pair of shoes in the millions that you produce surely does not warrant a lot of attention. But even though they may be only one pair in a million to you, they are one pair in three to me.

My others are a pair of Adidas sneakers and an old pair of Dockers. (Which get double duty now). So you see, to have one third of my "fleet" ailing, causes me some concern. I would like to know what I should do to stop the squeaking or even if I can.

Should I let the dogs rip them off my feet and chew them to bits, (as they would like to), boil them in oil, or drop them off at a cobbler? I know this must be one of those tasks which are probably considered an annoyance, but it is still important to me. They are by far my favorite shoes as they allow for much more freedom of movement then the

53

FLORSHEIM SHOES

Dockers and are much more appropriate then the
Adidas to wear while conducting our church choir.
No other shoes allow me to jump, kick, and twirl
like yours.

Please get back to me soon, I would like to
at least attempt a repair before our annual
"Hallelujah Halloween Concert." (It would be an
excellent effect during the haunted house sequence
but the sound man's union will not allow me to
overstep my bounds as a conductor. Pardon the pun.)
If you did not get, or misplaced my previous e-
mail, I would be happy to send it again. Just let
me know.

Thanks

Jackson Snead

REPLY

From: Florsheim Shoes
To: Jackson Snead
Sent: Wednesday, October 13, 2004
Subject: RE: Walker Texas Mouse-Killer

Dear Snead,

I apologize - but I was unable to locate the original email you sent
me. I conducted a search under your name, which is the only thing I
have to go by here, but I came up empty. Please resend your original
request, and I would gladly look into it.

FLORSHEIM SHOES

Regards,

Nicole Smith
International Customer Service and
Sales Administration Manage

REPLY

From: Jackson Snead
To: Nicole Smith
Sent: Saturday, October 2, 2003
Subject: Walker Texas Mouse-Killer

Dear Florsheim,

I have a pair of shoes manufactured by you which I
purchased about a year ago. I have worn the shoes
quite often for everything from working to dancing
to walking the dog. They are quite comfortable and
appropriate for many situations. (It is the black
Lido, I looked it up on your web site.)

Recently though, they have developed a squeak. Not
just a small squeak, but a loud, boisterous, high
pitched, squealing, alarming, yelping noise. It
sounds like I'm stomping mice. I can no longer wear
the shoes to work because they become the center
of attention whenever I walk across our showroom
floor, not to mention the jokes that I have to
endure. Canary-toes, Hamster-squeezer, the Squeak-

FLORSHEIM SHOES

meister, Walker Texas mouse-killer are just a few of my new nicknames. Now I only wear them when I walk the dog.

Actually, it comes in handy because dogs are fascinated by the noise. You should see the flurry of activity if I run!

Yet, as popular as I am with the dogs, I would like to fix the problem and be able to wear the shoes again to work. I heard that soaking them in WD-40 would do it, but I am reluctant to gamble on an urban myth solution. (I didn't do too good with the jet engine strapped to my Camaro, so now I check things out first)

...a loud, boisterous, high pitched, squealing, alarming, yelping noise. It sounds like I'm stomping mice.

That's why I am writing to you. I am probably not the first person to inquire for a solution to this problem and I am sure that your knowledgeable and friendly staff would have a multitude of cures at their fingertips. So what should I do?

Sincerely,
Jackson Snead

FLORSHEIM SHOES

REPLY

From: Nicole Smith
To: Jackson Snead
Sent: Thursday, October 14, 2004
Subject: RE: Walker Texas Mouse-Killer

Hi, Jackson

Where are you located?

Regards, Nicole Smith
International Customer Service and
Sales Administration Manager

REPLY

From: Jackson Snead
To: Nicole Smith
Sent: Friday, October 15, 2004
Subject: RE: Walker Texas Mouse-Killer

Dear Nicole

Thank you for your interest in me, I am located in
Victoria, BC. Our church is located at the foot
of Wharf St. If you are coming to see me, please
let me know and I will clean out the spare bedroom
for you. If you can make it for the Hallelujah
Halloween Concert I'm sure you will have a good
time. It turns out that I may perform in bare feet

FLORSHEIM SHOES

this year. Not just
because of the shoe
thing, but also because
I am going as a carp
and they don't wear
shoes.

Let me know ASAP, there
are very few tickets
still available. You don't want to miss Wallace
Bernstein's version of "Old Man, Old Bag". It's a
showstopper.

Jackson

REPLY

From: Nicole Smith
To: Tyson Cameron ; Jackson Snead
Sent: Friday, October 15, 2004
Subject: RE: Walker Texas Mouse-Killer

Hi Jackson,

I was actually in Vancouver on vacation last week... I love British
Columbia. It's one of my favorite places!!

Florsheim in Canada is serviced exclusively through our licensee,
S&S Imports, located in Toronto.

I'm referring your email to Tyson in their office for review. You should
hear from him soon.

FLORSHEIM SHOES

Thanks again for taking the time to contact us!

Regards,

Nicole Smith
International Customer Service and
Sales Administration Manager

REPLY

From: Jackson Snead
To: Nicole Smith
Sent: Saturday, October 16, 2004
Subject: RE: Walker Texas Mouse-Killer

Hi Nicole,

Gee, how coincidental that you were in Vancouver
last week. I should have written a week earlier
and we could have met up. I could have shown you
my shoes. I like Vancouver too, but you have to
go pretty far to beat Victoria. The only place
that comes to mind is a small island in the South
Pacific, Pomeratu. If you ever get a chance, you
should go there.

I don't think they have many shoes, but you might
find something else you like just as much. They
have big snails. Anyway, I sure appreciate all
your help. I'll let you know how it goes. If your
squeaky shoe cure does not work, I may try a few

FLORSHEIM SHOES

things myself. After all, I am kind of a scientist.

Just out of curiosity, what city are you in? I would have guessed Baltimore until you said you were in Vancouver. Now I think I'll guess Spokane. I'll bet you really get around being in one of those big international shoe companies. Ever been to Moscow in the winter? Now those are some serious shoes!

To bad you are going to miss our concert.

Jackson

REPLY

From: Nicole Smith
To: Jackson Snead
Sent: Monday, October 18, 2004
Subject: RE: Walker Texas Mouse-Killer

Hi Jackson,

We're in Milwaukee, Wisconsin...

Regards,

Nicole Smith
International Customer Service and
Sales Administration Manager

FLORSHEIM SHOES

From: Tyson Cameron
To: Jackson Snead
Sent: Tuesday, October 19, 2004
Subject: RE: Walker Texas Mouse-Killer

Jackson,

Thank you for your continued interest in Florsheim¨. I apologize for the delay in a response but I have been out of the office. In response to your inquiry, please return the shoes to the retailer that they were purchased or take the shoes to a local shoe maker and advise us of his comments. After we know what exactly is wrong with the shoe, we will be better able to assist you. If you have any further questions/comments/concerns, please do not hesitate to contact me.

Best regards,

Tyson Cameron
Florsheim¨ Canada

REPLY

From: Jackson Snead
To: Tyson Cameron
Sent: Sunday, October 24, 2004
Subject: RE: Walker Texas Mouse-Killer

Dear Tyson,

61

FLORSHEIM SHOES

Thanks for your reply to my inquiry. Were you in Vancouver too like your associate, Nicole? That would just be too much of a coincidence. Anyway, I have booked an appointment with the local shoe doctor for early next week as you advised. It turns out that one of the more creative members of my choir group will be using my shoes for a special squeaky sneaky sequence during our Hallelujah Halloween Concert on Sunday, so it kind of worked out that the shoes squeak right now. (I don't know if Nicole told you about the concert, but I am the Choir master for the event.) So thanks for your interest, and I'll let you know what the doctor says next week.

Jackson

From: Jackson Snead
To: Nicole Smith
Sent: Sunday, October 24, 2004
Subject: RE: Walker Texas Mouse-Killer

Hi Nicole,

Tyson got back to me the other day, and I have booked an appointment with the local shoe doctor for a diagnosis next week.

Turns out that the sound man's union doesn't care

FLORSHEIM SHOES

if we use squeaky shoes for effect, so we have
created a special sneaky squeaky shoe segment. It
is sure to bring the house down tonight! The punch
line coincides with a pumpkin explosion and results
in the sneaky squeaker being knocked out of his
shoes. (good thing this pair is the slip on Lidos
or it wouldn't be near as funny). Anyhow, I hope
things are good in Milwaukee for Halloween and
that you don't have to put up with too many Richie
Cunninghams chasing Laverne and Shirley through
the brewery as they sing about happy days. Isn't
that Seventies Show situated there too? It seems
every time I see something about Milwaukee, it's a
different year. And I thought it was hard enough
to keep on top of Daylight Savings Time. It's 2004
here on the coast, what year is it there?

Jackson

From: Jackson Snead
To: Tyson Cameron
Sent: Wednesday, October 27, 2004
Subject: RE: Walker Texas Mouse-Killer

Dear Tyson,

I went to the shoe doctor today to get an initial
inspection and diagnosis of the squeak problem.
The shoe doctor is a recent immigrant from Papua-
New Guinea on an exchange program with other

FLORSHEIM SHOES

practitioners of the orthopedic profession. He
calls himself Mr. Boots. Anyway, he was fascinated
by the problem and eagerly took them back to his
workshop, where I heard loud and enthusiastic
pounding. After about half an hour he emerged
triumphant and presented me with the shoes.
Unfortunately, because of the language barrier, he
had misunderstood me and given the other shoe a
squeak as well.

Apparently, in Papua-New Guinea, it is considered
a sign of good luck and high social status to have
squeaky shoes. (It's probably a mark of high status
just to have shoes there.)

Then he told me that if I didn't want them to
squeak, I should put them on a goat, since it was
obvious to him that they would not squeak if worn
by a goat.

I think that was some kind of Papua-New Guinea
insult. So, anyway, now I have two shoes that

FLORSHEIM SHOES

squeak in harmony and Mr Boot's footprint on my
butt. I think I will go to the German Shoemaker
down the road next.

I'll let you know how that goes.

Jackson

REPLY

From: Nicole Smith
To: Jackson Snead
Sent: Wednesday, November 3, 2004
Subject: RE: Walker Texas Mouse-Killer

Hi Jackson,

I took extra time off for Halloween... Things in Milwaukee were very
good this year - it's really Madison that has all the riots and stuff!
That 70's show is in Milwaukee, and there was another show some
years ago called Step By Step with Patrick Duffy & Suzanne Somers
that was set in Port Washington, which is just a little north of us. It is
really 2004 here! And currently, my office is all a-buzz with Election
Talk - it's been a very exciting day!!

Regards, Nicole Smith
International Customer Service and
Sales Administration Manager
Weyco Group, Inc.

FLORSHEIM SHOES

REPLY

From: Jackson Snead
To: Nicole Smith
Sent: Monday, November 15, 2004
Subject: No More Squeakin'

Hi Nicole
Sorry it took a while to get back to you, but I was just released this morning. Most of the charges have been dropped and my lawyer says there is very little chance of me going to jail. So if you saw the headlines, (I don't know how far they went,) I am not a crazed choir-master who tried to blow his audience to kingdom come.

I am not trying to follow in the footsteps of cult-meister Jim Jones or those sneaker wearing Californians a few years ago. And I tell you what, I am never, ever, ever, going to ask the troubled teens from the halfway house to prepare the exploding pumpkins again.

I should have suspected something when they insisted on standing at the back of the church, and when they laughed too much when the sneaky squeaker made his appearance in the skit, and it probably wouldn't have been to late to stop it when I saw them all duck behind the pews just before the explosion.

Most of the people in the front few rows, (where

FLORSHEIM SHOES

you would have been sitting as my guest) have got
their hearing back now, and Ralph Emerson (who
played the sneaky squeaker) was brought down from
the roof of the neighboring warehouse without a
scratch by the firefighters shortly after the main
fire was put out.

Anyway, as you can imagine, this has delayed
my appointment with the shoe doctor, (who said
he would have to bill me anyway for the missed
appointment) but I did have the presence of mind
to recover my shoes from the orchestra pit before
fleeing the rubble. On the brighter side, the skit
did bring the house down, and now we can rebuild
the stage area as we have wanted to for years.

I hope Christmas goes a bit smoother.

Jackson

IMPERIAL TOBACCO

CIGARETTE DETECTIVE

From: Jackson Snead
To; Imperial Tobacco
Sent: Friday, August 13, 2004
Subject: Cigarette Detective

Dear Sirs,

The other day I purchased a pack of cigarettes which looked like yours, but were clearly of an inferior quality. Several reliable sources tell me that they were American Tobacco. I suspect it may be part of that counterfeit cigarette smuggling ring that I hear about on TV.

I don't really know which store I purchased it at but I could retrace my steps for you and probably point it out if you are interested.

Anyway, I thought you should know that there are some inferior identical products out there and you probably need to change your packaging to keep ahead of the counterfeiters.

Along those lines, I had an idea the other day about how to create a bit more of a positive buzz about your product. Remember the talking beer cans that said "you are a winner"? Well, you could have a cigarette pack that spoke when you opened it. It would be a lot easier to manufacture because it's not submerged in a beer can. You could have it say something that

68

IMPERIAL TOBACCO

shows you do care about people's health. Something like "Don't forget to take your vitamins." or "Don't forget to pray today", or even "Eat your vegetables".

I'm sure the government may want to have their say about this too, they might suggest something like, "I'm gonna kill ya" or, "I'll rip your lungs out, Jim"

You might have to give away something lame too, so as not to encourage people to get too enthusiastic about your product. But hey, people love to win anything; you could give them a free funeral and they'd love it. Everyone has already received their free coughin' so it would all be part of the same theme.

You can have that idea for free. You don't have to pay me or anything. I think you guys make an excellent cigarette, and if the government has dirty hands by participating in tax revenues from your product then they ought to leave you guys alone in the courts. Like my Daddy used to say, "If you are swimming in the same pool, then you're drinking the same pee."

So what do you think? Should I track down the counterfeiters for you? Let me know.

Thanks,
Jackson

IMPERIAL TOBACCO

REPLY

From: Imperial Tobacco
To: Jackson Snead
Sent: Tuesday, August 17, 2004
Subject: Cigarette Detective

Dear Mr. Snead,

Thank you for your e-mail. Your comments are much appreciated. Yes, if it is possible for you to track down where you purchased this pack, it would be helpful to us. If you still have the pack, would it be possible to mail to us? 3711 St-Antoine, Montreal, QC H4C 3P6.

As far as give aways or contests, etc. are concerned, the federal Tobacco Act prohibits such activities as they are construed as promotional.

Thank you for your interest.

Sincerely,

Mary Fornier
Public Affairs

REPLY

From: Jackson Snead
To: Imperial Tobacco
Sent: Wednesday, August 18, 2004
Subject: Cigarette Detective

Dear Mary,

Thanks for your quick response to my inquiry.
I think it's important that we all do our part
to reduce crime, and I am thrilled to have been

IMPERIAL TOBACCO

deputized by you to go out and track down those criminals. I am going to purchase a small video camera to document the event. I am also watching reruns of The Rockford Files and the Pink Panther films to prepare.

Since the store was in Vancouver and I am in Victoria, it will be several days before I have an address for you. One good thing about this is that many more people over there have tattoo's on their face so I won't stand out like a sore thumb.

I may have to purchase several cartons of real packs to get to the counterfeits so you may have to be patient with me if it takes a while. But rest assured, I take these things very seriously and I'll do what it takes. I guess I should have sent you some of the original package that I purchased but they are so damn addictive that I smoked them all within a couple of hours.

Proud to serve,

Jackson Snead

REPLY

From: Imperial Tobacco
To: Jackson Snead
Sent: Thursday, August 19, 2004
Subject: Cigarette Detective

Dear Sir,

Thank you again for your interest
However, as this happened in
another city, it may be just as wel

IMPERIAL TOBACCO

to let it go as we would not want you to incur any expenses tracking this down. Your offer is much appreciated nonetheless.

Sincerely,

Mary Fornier
Public Affairs

REPLY

From: Jackson Snead
To: Imperial Tobacco
Sent: Thursday, August 19, 2004
Subject: Cigarette Detective

Dear Mary,

Thanks for your concern about my financial situation, but as JFK said, "It is for the betterment of mankind that I commit to justice." I've got to smoke anyway, so it doesn't matter if I do it in Vancouver or Victoria. And I have already made the plans to proceed with this investigation, to stop it now would be more costly. I can return the video camera to London Drugs within 30 days anyhow.

I'll keep you informed of my progress. I'm booked on the 1pm ferry so I'm leaving now and I'll contact you when I have something to report.

Here's to a successful investigation,

Jackson Snead

IMPERIAL TOBACCO

REPLY

From: Jackson Snead
To: Imperial Tobacco
Sent: Sunday, September 5, 2004
Subject: Cigarette Detective

Dear Mary,

Sorry I took so long to get back to you, but I have been doing a bang-up job for you as you will see by the notes of the investigation. I was successful, I believe, in obtaining the counterfeit cigarettes and am forwarding them to you via post as requested. It was obvious by not only the taste, but the packaging that they were counterfeits. The plastic was wrapped way too loose and the stamp just fell off.

They also sell real cigarettes at this store, so I had to purchase many packs over the period of a couple of weeks to get some counterfeits. I was further detained by the Police as they had some concerns about the video camera and it's contents. Perhaps after you finish my report, you could send a short note to Special Investigator Albert Swinehinderson at <u>Albertswinehindersontheman@</u> <u>hotmail.com</u> to confirm
that I was on a case
for you. I could
probably get most of
the charges dropped
if he saw that I was
on the level. I will

IMPERIAL TOBACCO

probably also get the camera back and then be able
to return it to London Drugs.

Here is the log that I kept of the investigation
for you.

__Investigators Log__

Day 1, I am filled with excitement to be going to Vancouver on a case. I will blend in with the local population, gain their trust and infiltrate the counterfeit organization. I will learn their ways, their secret mannerisms, and find out where their soft underbelly lies. Then, like a fire ant, I will strike. Tonight I set up camp near the store. I begin by making a purchase tomorrow.

Day 2, I have purchased several packs of cigarettes at the suspected store and am sampling them to determine if they are fakes. I have positioned myself in a bush near the loading door. I brought along my good friend, Jack Daniels to keep me company. No suspicious activity yet.

Day 3, I must have been whacked on the head from behind last night, I have a thundering headache and Jack is all gone. I will make another attempt to purchase the counterfeit cigarettes today.

Day 4, Have gone through probably 30 packs in the last few days. I must get more funds to complete the investigation. I have considered soliciting people on the street for money but they seem put off by the tattoo on my face. The store owner speaks an entirely different language. It's like he has a different word for almost everything. I don't think he trusts me yet. He does not want me to work there. Infiltrating his organization may be harder then first thought.

Day 5, Have run out of funds and am gathering butts from around the store to determine if they are fakes. Some taste pretty bad, but nothing definite yet.

74

IMPERIAL TOBACCO

Day 6, Bingo, I found one that was definitely American Tobacco. Now I just have to link it to the store. I will continue my surveillance by hanging around the corner and sniffing the air as smokers go by. There is no way I am going to be intimidated by Mohammed and his gang of thugs who keep threatening me.

Day 7, I have decided to take up another surveillance post on top of a hill a few blocks away. Although I do not have a clear view anymore of the store, I will probably make more progress if I stop arousing the store proprietor and aggravating his pit-bull. I do not have any spare pants with me, so I have had to adapt an old towel I found into a garment. Luckily, I was able to draw a tartan pattern on it so I look like a Scotsman. I have adopted the proper accent as well. This is where my preparation and skill come in. I will attempt a purchase again today.

Day 8, Apparently, it is illegal in Vancouver for people to express their own fashion sense and design their own clothes. The police have decided that a tea towel is not appropriate attire for walking the streets, especially if there is a playground nearby. They also did not like my surveillance post, bushes are not for hiding in they tell me. I am also told I will need confirmation from Imperial Tobacco that I was on a case before they release the video camera to me.

Day 9, Success!!!! I have purchased an American cigarette in a DuMaurier wrapper. I will be able to send this in as evidence. I think Jack and I will get together again tonight to celebrate. It is starting to rain, I will have to gather some boxes for shelter tonight.

Day 10, I smoked all the evidence again last night, spilled Jack, and burned down my shelter. Luckily, the rain put out the fire before it spread to the rest of the parking garage. Too bad about the Volkswagen. Now I have to find a new place to sleep and I will have to gather some money again to continue.

Day 11, Again success!!!!! I must have mastered his code. I have the fakes in hand.

IMPERIAL TOBACCO

Some compadres and I got enough money for a pack. We each get 5 cigarettes. Unfortunately, they do not feel compelled to send in any portion of theirs as evidence. I'm starting to get homesick now and I think my fish should be fed soon so I have decided to return to Victoria. I will put a package together for you and send it from there. I may have to smuggle myself on board a ferry to get home.

Day 12, Luckily, the BC Ferry security guys do not check the animal sections of livestock trucks as well as they should. I guess it's because of the smell. I must send in the cigarettes as evidence. I have only one left and some butts.

Day 13, I sent the package today. Here is the address of the store, it is the **Market at 9621 Queensway, Burnaby BC.** I am now safely at home and relaxing after my successful undercover operation. I will be catching some new fish today, the aquarium needed to be cleaned anyway. On the brighter side, I found my hairbrush. The fish smell should come out if I boil it for a few hours. You should get the counterfeit cigarettes in the mail soon, and that will give you the evidence you need to initiate your proceedings. I guess I'll let you guys take it from here.

```
Please don't forget about the e-mail to clear me.

Thanks,
Jackson Snead
```

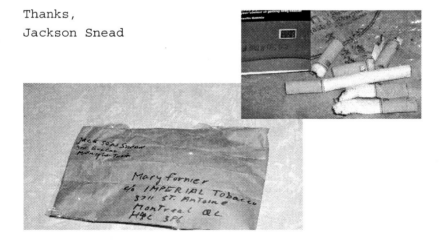

IMPERIAL TOBACCO

From: Jackson Snead
To: Imperial Tobacco
Sent: Sunday, September 12, 2004
Subject: Cigarette Detective

Dear Mary,

Just a quick note to confirm to you that the counterfeit cigarettes have been sent to you at your Montreal address via Canada Post.

You should get it very soon. I hope you are able to confirm to Special Investigator Swinehinderson that I was on a case for you. I only have a couple more days when I can return the camera or I have to pay for it.

If you did not get my previous e-mail with the address of the store and Mr. Swinehinderson's address just let me know and I will forward it to you again.

Thanks,
Jackson Snead

IMPERIAL TOBACCO

From: Albert Swinehinderson
<albertswinehindersontheman@hotmail.com
To: Imperial Tobacco
Sent: Wednesday, September 15, 2004
Subject: *PLEASE CONFIRM THIS IS REAL*

Dear Mary Fornier,

Can you please confirm that you sent this E-mail to
Mr. Snead as he claims on August 17, 2004:

> Dear Mr. Snead
> Thank you for your e-mail. Your comments are much
> appreciated. Yes, if it is possible for you to track down where
> you purchased this pack, it would be helpful to us. If you
> still have the pack, would it be possible to mail to us? 3711
> St-Antoine, Montreal, QC H4C 3P6. As far as give aways or
> contests, etc. are concerned, the federal Tobacco Act prohibits
> such activities as they are construed as promotional.
>
> Thank you for your interest.
> Sincerely,
> Mary Fornier
> Public Affairs

Your cooperation is appreciated.
Thank You,

Special Investigator,
Albert Swinehinderson

78

IMPERIAL TOBACCO

From: Jackson Snead
To: Imperial Tobacco
Sent: Saturday, September 18, 2004
Subject: Cigarette Detective

Dear Mary,

I guess you must be on holidays as I have not heard
back from you yet. I hope you get back soon because
no one believes I was working for you. I sent the
cigarettes last week and you should have them by
now. There was only one fully intact cigarette and
a couple of butts. I thought you might be able to
tell from the filter if it was one of yours. It
seems that one of my friends might have slipped
one of his own rollie butts into the plastic wrap
when I wasn't looking. If you found a butt that was
obviously hand rolled, just throw it away. It was
not supposed to go to you and will definitely not
be DuMaurier tobacco. It may not even be tobacco.
So just ignore it and throw it away. I was really
pissed at him for undermining my credibility like
that. He's not coming over anymore when I have a
serious job to do.

Let me know when you get them, ok?

Jackson Snead

IMPERIAL TOBACCO

REPLY

From: Imperial Tobacco
To: Jackson Snead
Sent: Monday, September 20, 2004
Subject: Cigarette Detective

Dear Mr. Snead,

We just received your envelope and are very appreciative of all
the trouble you went to. We will forward this information, location
of store and cigarette and butts, to the appropriate channels and
as you say - let them take it from here! Yes, we have e-mailed Mr.
Swinehinderson to confirm your involvement. Thank you again for
your log of activities, it made for very interesting reading.

Yours truly,
Mary Fornier

From: Imperial Tobacco
To: Albert Swinehinderson
Sent: Monday, September 20, 2004
Subject: Jackson Snead
Dear Sir,

Mr. Snead did e-mail us saying he thought he had purchased a
counterfeit product. We did respond that if it was not complicated and
if it did not mean incurring expenses he could try to track it down
for us. We appreciate all his efforts and yours if you were involved in
any way.

Thank you again.
Mary Fornier
Consultant, Public Affairs

IMPERIAL TOBACCO

From: Albert Swinehinderson
<albertswinehindersontheman@hotmail.com>
To: Imperial Tobacco
Sent: Tuesday, September 21, 2004
Subject: Jackson Snead

Dear Mary,

Thank you for the confirmation regarding Jackson Snead. You will be glad to know that we have dropped most of the charges against your associate.

We are not sure of the nature of the professional relationship that you enjoy with Mr. Snead, but it does not appear to contravene any laws.

We have reviewed and released the videotape as well. Mr. Snead assures me that you will be quite interested in it.

I personally hope not.

Good Luck,

Special Investigator
Albert Swinehinderson

IMPERIAL TOBACCO

From: Jackson Snead
To: Imperial Tobacco
Sent: Friday, September 24, 2004
Subject: Contract Offer

Dear Mary,

You'll be happy to know that your confirmation was like a get out of jail free card. I got back both bags of stuff.

Although, you will be disappointed to hear that I had to settle up with London Drugs for the camera. Apparently, melting is not a manufacturing defect or covered under warranty.

Anyway, I am glad to have been of assistance in uncovering the smuggling ring. If you have another assignment, I'd be happy to help. Although, I think I would have to get some kind of pay. Say, 2 million a year. (That's just a first offer, you can counter and see if I go for it.)

You might consider paying me in smokes if you want. I can always trade them for food and services. I only have this little misunderstanding about the length of the "kilt" to iron out now, and I'll be able to leave the province again.

Next time I'll wear a Toga.

Jackson Snead

VISA

VANCOUVER ISLAND SEPARATION ASSOCIATION

From: Jackson Snead
Sent: Sunday, March 6, 2005
To: Ask Visa Canada
Subject: Thanks for your assistance

Vancouver Island Separation Association

Dear VISA

A few months ago my associate wrote to you regarding the use of some of your artwork and stationary for our fledgling political party, of the same name, VISA. (Vancouver Island Separation Association) We got no response from you which I am sure indicated acceptance of our request and policies.

This is most generous of you, and as pointed out in our previous letter, you stand to benefit greatly from the publicity and financial policies of our party. (All government transactions will be done on VISA cards)

VISA

To bring you up to date with our progress, we recently held a party convention at which a high profile Canadian celebrity was named party leader.

We will release his or her name once all the papers are signed and accepted. But rest assured, it will make international headlines, guaranteeing VISA widespread publicity. Both of us. As well, all the posters and flyers are done, using the VISA logo. We didn't have to change a thing to the old VISA signs that we found as it was just perfect. Some party participants wanted to change the colors, but once cost was discussed, they went with your original colors and designs.

Our signature drive has collected about 1.3 million signatures on the island, which represents a huge slice of the population. (Some still need to be verified.) Very few dogs were released on our canvassers, and only one injury was reported. (It was in the staunchly federalist riding of crabby old men in Oak Bay and we expected it.)

Anyway, people are surprised that we are aligned corporately and politically, but we just point out that we are above the board with our alliances and will always give people the straight goods.

They seem to appreciate that. So right now, we are running into a bit of a funding crisis as payment is due on the party's mountain retreat and we are asking our corporate sponsors for a contribution to delay the foreclosure proceedings. Not much is needed; only $75,000 and that

VISA

will clear title. That would
allow us to plant our roots and
secure our political base.
Of course if you donate the
majority of the money, it
will be called the VISA
center. You will make far more
than that in the first week of our
governments tenure, and even more when
we run up the interest charges and late
fees. We are hoping that you will find it in
your budget to assist us, as we would hate to have
to call it the Save-On-Foods Center for the VISA
party. Or worse, the MasterCard Center for the VISA
Party. We haven't even asked American Express for
obvious reasons.

Please get back to me quickly as the election is
expected to be called soon.

Hoping to make a card deal,
Jackson Snead

REPLY

From: "Ask Visa"
To: "Jackson Snead"
Sent: Tuesday, March 8, 2005
Subject: 17SD RE: Thanks for your assistance
Dear Jackson Snead:

Thank you for your inquiry. I have forwarded your message to VISA's
Legal and Marketing areas for their attention.

Thank you for writing.
VISA Canada Webmaster

VISA

From: VISA
To: Jackson Snead
Sent: Friday, March 11, 2005
Subject: Request Denied

Dear Mr. Snead:

We respond to your inquiry received through our Ask Visa Canada mailbox. We are not in receipt of the initial letter you speak of, requesting consent to use Visa's artwork and stationery for your activities.

Moreover, we have not identified anyone in Vancouver who is familiar with the Vancouver Island Separation Association -- although the number of signatures you mention would be roughly 65% of the population of the greater Vancouver area. In the end, we must decline your proposal and your request to use Visa's trademarks for your activities.

Incidentally, as you know, Visa owns several trademarks including "VISA" and the "VISA & Bands Design" marks and has registered them worldwide (including in Canada). Visa cannot grant you permission to use any Visa-owned mark -- or anything confusingly similar to them.

Therefore, we ask that you and the Vancouver Island Separation Association refrain from using or immediately stop using any and all Visa-owned marks.

Sincerely,

Visa Webmaster

VISA

REPLY

Dear Visa,

In response to your letter regarding your support for our fledgling political party, VISA, Vancouver Island Separation Association, I must write to clarify a few points.

First though, I must apologize for our party membership figure which I quoted. I misplaced a comma. The correct figure should have read 13,000. It is not surprising that your poll of Vancouver did not reveal widespread knowledge of our party yet as we have yet to make big headlines.

That will come when we announce our Canadian celebrity leader. Another reason for our low profile over there is that Vancouverites rarely think past the city limits when thinking of BC. Hence the entire reason for our party.

Anyway, I am still a little foggy on what you are trying to tell me in your letter. Are you saying that you are limiting your assistance to us a party? Will there be less financial assistance coming than we expected?

And what about your trademark? How will that work when we obviously have the same name? I

87

VISA

thought this had all been
straightened out by my associate
with you, and you had agreed that
in return for the use of your
card by us exclusively as a financial
instrument, you would provide the logo
and necessary stationary. The whole purpose
of this arrangement was to make VISA synonymous
with VISA. Thereby ensuring your monopoly in our
little kingdom. It can only work to your benefit,
and bring you lots of business. I think you may
have misinterpreted our intentions. We have no
intentions of introducing any kind of competing
product or credit card , unless you want the VISA
VISA.

Anyway, I hope we can continue the friendly
relationship and get the wrinkles ironed out before
the election is called. We stand a very good chance
of running this province after the incumbent
nutballs shoot their feet off again. Soon we will
be the only choice among rational people.

Sincerely,
Jackson Snead

THE TELEPHONE CALL FROM VISA'S LAWYER

Hello, is Mr. Snead there?

Yes, speaking.

Mr. Snead, my name is Ken Van der Law and I would like to get some information about the Vancouver Island Separation Association.

VISA

Sure, How did you find out about us?

Well, a Friend told me about you.

Oh, that's interesting, and what was your friends name?

Well, that's not all that important right now, I'm just trying to find out a bit about your organization.

Oh, Ok, Where are you calling from?

I'm calling from Toronto.

Wow, I didn't know that anyone in Toronto even heard about our group before. What did you say your friends name was.

Well, actually it's my employer that wants to find out about your group.

Oh, who do you work for?

Well, I am actually a lawyer in a firm in Toronto.

Wow, and who are you asking questions for now?

I'm actually working for VISA right now.

Cool, I like VISA.

Would you mind answering a few questions about your group for my report?

No not at all, what would you like to know?

Well, first of all, how big is your group?

It varies, depending on the size of the table, but generally about 6 to eight, but on Thursday night when they have two for one beer night we can get up to 20-25.

VISA

I thought your letter said there was several thousand involved?

Yeah, we were drunk when we started counting and it's a round table.

I couldn't find any registration of your party name when I searched the political parties of BC. Are you registered?

No, not yet, we have to get the right name still. We can't go registering the VISA party if you are going to sue us right away, can we? We may have to change our name to VIP (Vancouver Island Party) anyway because we have been trying to get Pamela Anderson to be our celebrity leader and we thought she would be more likely to join us if we changed our name to the same name as her show.

What kind of platform are you running on?

We haven't even figured that out yet, but we do know we'll need credit. We just thought we would create a bit of a buzz and see what people wanted before we said anything. We figure if we don't say anything at all, people will just vote for us because Pam's our leader. She's a lot easier to look at then anyone else in the campaign. Wouldn't you agree?

Yes, you do have a point there. So do you expect to have a high profile in this coming election?

Oh, I don't know, Pam still hasn't got back to us if she wants the job yet, so we might not do anything this time. We are getting pretty close to election time now and we may have missed our window of opportunity. We might have to place a call to Valdy if we don't get a response soon. Do you think Visa is going to sue us?

That's not really up to me. I don't make those decisions.

Oh, OK, Well, do you think we have done anything illegal yet?

I can't really say.

Would you vote for Pam?

VISA

Again, hard to say.

I'll take that as a yes . Any chance you would like to make a donation to our party?

No, I think I've spent just about enough already and I think I have all I need to complete my report.

OK, well, keep in touch then.

You can count on that. Bye Now.

Bye bye.

REPLY

From: Jackson Snead
To: VISA LAWYER
Sent: Wednesday, May 11, 2005 8:57 AM
Subject: VISA Trademarks

Dear Ken,

Thanks for your prompt, no nonsense approach to our situation. I appreciate straight talk more than most people. Although our group has suffered it's share of setbacks in the last week, and we are down to the last few days before the election, we are still hopeful of some recognition. I am somewhat disappointed by a lack of response from Pamela Anderson (our most famous hometown-girl) with regards to her leadership position within our party, but we can probably still go with Valdy. Preliminary polling gave Pamela about a 95% popular vote for premier so we felt it was a shoe-in if she accepted our nomination. (Only the waitress wouldn't vote for her.) Anyway, we are probably looking towards the next election

91

VISA

now unless Pam magically appears, as in episode 31 of V.I.P. Regardless, we still have the party name and identity issue to work out. From our conversation, I understand that VISA does not want us to use their name and colors. I fully understand but am disappointed. We still have all those VISA signs that were found in the basement of a gas station in Bowser that would be perfect with some slight alteration. I wonder if you could clarify for me what parameters would constitute trademark infringement with regards to the name and colors. Can we not use the word: VISA, or any derivative of it, such as VISAS or SVISA or TVISA?

What about the colors, are the trademarked colors restricted to the blue and gold? What about other shades of blue and gold or if I add another color to the mix such as green? Is it only the combination of the name and colors together that represent an infringement?

Please understand that this is not meant to antagonize you but these are all questions that have been put to me by other party members and require clarification before we can move ahead.

Thanks for your help,

Jackson Snead
Vancouver Island Separation Association

PS, We don't really advocate separation, just in case you were wondering.

PAMELA ANDERSON

PAM FOR PREMIER

From: Jackson Snead
To: Pamela Anderson
Sent: Tuesday, April 5, 2005
Subject: Pam for Premier

Dear Pam,

I am writing to inform you of your nomination to become British Columbia's next Premier. Our fledgling political party is sure you could help us win the election this May. We all voted for you at our leadership convention and advance polling suggests a landslide victory for you and our party.

Could you please respond as we would like to finalize the press release.

Judging by the performances of the Premiers of the past, you would not have to do much and it would probably not affect your everyday life.

We really would like you to lead our party.

Thank you for your consideration,

Jackson Snead
Vancouver Island Separation Association

PAMELA ANDERSON

Since there was no reply from the recipients of this email, I offer the following

Manufactured Suggested Reply

Dear Jackson,

I'd love to be premieress of BC. I would be perfect for the job. I don't know anything about politics or running a province, but Prince Everhard of the Netherlands has offered to teach me a thing or two about keeping a firm hand on the staff of power without being a dictator. I'm sure I could assemble a huge caucus of willing participants to help me. From my own friends, I have Jack Hoff and his buddy, Johnny Jump-up. Then there is Private Parts, Sergeant Stiffy, Major Woody, Admiral Winky and Chief of Staff, Longrod Von Hugenstein who can help out with military matters. On the environmental side, fisherman's friend and master bait man Willie Wanker has offered to be an upright citizen and keep track of the zipper trout population trying to make it to Happy Canyon. My pets, Ralphy, the fur-faced chicken is excited to be moving into new digs in lotus land and doing a little oyster shucking while Honk, the Magic Goose, is practicing pecking her whisker biscuit so she doesn't embarrass herself with bad table manners when she is in the public eye. Old Blind Bob and the Twins have offered to bring out their instruments and jam at the inaugural ball and Uncle Wiggly has promised to go straight if I win. I hear there is a huge swell of support for me. Hopefully, things will go really well, but I could always let my blouse bunnies loose if I need a distraction during a press conference. I'm sure I would be an improvement over the premiers that came before me, because like Chi Zi Wang says, 'Two boobs are better than one.'

Pam

BC FERRIES

FREEDOM FERRY

From: Jackson Snead
To: BC Ferries
Sent: Sunday, July 13, 2003
Subject: Freedom Ferry

Dear BC Ferries,

I would like to thank you for creating the most comfortable traveling environment that I have ever experienced. I have traveled extensively on trains, buses, planes, even donkey carts, and there has never been better and more forgiving seating arrangements for my condition then your ferries. I suffer from a rare form of gastro intestinal effluvium, or chronic gas.

I find that when I travel by all other modes of transportation, my condition becomes the subject of attention within minutes. Either someone comments on the gathering storm clouds or starts looking under their seats for "something left behind" (European train compartments are the worst.) I find I can travel on your ferries and "express" myself as needed and because of the variety of areas and large compartments, no-one is the wiser. Having lived with this condition for nearly 20 years, (since I was detained in a Kenyan Jail for suspicious activities and spent 10 days

95

eating rhinoceros stew,) I have learned to "release the pressure" quietly and in such a way as to steer the blame away from myself. Unfortunately, this condition causes not only the production of excess gas, but probably the foulest odor you can imagine. (People often think there is a rotting whale nearby.) As you can imagine, it does not go unnoticed.

I find that the variety of areas, kids play areas, reading sections, cafeteria sections, outside areas, and the combination of your food menu, make it possible for no-one to suspect that the odor emanates from within me. (It is a little less convincing since the disappearance of the Sunshine Breakfast, but I haven't been fingered yet.) Riding BC Ferries has become one of my favorite things to do just so that I feel accepted and normal in society. When you live with this kind of an affliction people only want to make fun of it and make up names for you. I have heard them all. (Radio guru Howard Stern created Fart-Man after I sat beside him on an airplane once. I take private pleasure in the fact that I grossed him out.)

So anyway, I want to thank you for creating the most comfortable travel environment that I have ever been in. I do not feel like a freak when on board and I am treated with all the respect of any other passenger. (I travel on the ferry about 8 times a week and sometimes on weekends just for the relief.) I also have a few question to ask of you. I am part of a support group for people with my affliction and we meet once a month somewhere in the lower mainland.

There are relatively few places that will allow

BC FERRIES

us to gather anymore for obvious reasons. We have decided that it would be appropriate for us to meet on the ferry. There are about 150 of us and we will be wearing small pink buttons that say POOT on them so that you can identify us among the normal people. We would like to catch the ferry in Tsawassen to Swartz Bay, where we will be joined by other members of the group from the island. We will then hold the bulk of our meeting on the return trip to Tsawassen after which the mainlanders will disembark and the islanders then go back to the island. This means that we will be on three consecutive sailings. We do not want to disembark with the other passengers after each leg of the journey as the ferry is our real destination.

(It would waste time and possibly interrupt some of the skits that we usually perform for our enjoyment during our meetings.)Also, could you brew a special coffee for us? We will provide it. It is called

We usually avoid spicy food.

BC FERRIES

Kopi Luwak, which is a very expensive but delicious coffee from Indonesia. It is our one indulgence at our meetings. Could you please tell us how to purchase the appropriate tickets for the return trips, and which sailings and ship you would prefer us to utilize. We would prefer one of the bigger ferries so we can blend in easier. With any luck, you will never even know we are on board.

Please respond to me quickly as I need to inform the other members for our regular end of the month meeting.

Thank You,
Jackson Snead

From: Jackson Snead
To: BC Ferries
Sent: Sunday, July 20, 2003
Subject: Freedom Ferry

Dear Ferries

Last week I sent an inquiry regarding having our meeting aboard your vessel. (Survivors of gastro-effluvium disorder). I have enclosed the previous e-mail for your remembrance at the end of this missive. I hope I can get an answer quickly because of our short deadline. It would be quite disruptive to our regular agenda to have to disembark, then re-board again during our support group. I do not want to have your onboard staff wondering why all these people are not getting off the ferry as usual, and I do not want to cause any concern regarding the odor that may permeate the ferry during our voyage.

If you find it inconvenient to brew our special
blend of coffee, I understand. I could have my
man-servant (Short-stuff) brew it for us and
accompany us during the voyage. He is a little
person and so he comes by his name honestly. He
will be dressed in his usual red velvet attire. We
do need to know if there is anyplace where he can
plug in a large coffee-maker if this is to be the
case. We would like to find out if it is possible
to remain on board during normal disembarkment
periods though. That is of the utmost concern to
me, as this is my month to prepare the agenda.

If we have to disembark we may need to stay on
board for a couple more crossings.

Thank You,
Jackson Snead

Keeping a calm and nonchalant demeanor is essential to maintaining an air of innocence.

BC FERRIES

REPLY

From: "Parson, Max D BCF:EX"
To: Jackson Snead
Subject: #20406 Jackson Snead;
Date: Thursday, July 24, 2003

Hello Jackson.

Thank you for your e-mail. I'm sorry we have no record of your earlier e-mail, so I appreciate your including a copy of it with your latest note. I admit I was unsure, having read your note, whether it is intended to be taken seriously. Perhaps you are familiar with this reaction. I have forwarded your requests to the appropriate manager with a request to contact you and see what can be done to accommodate your requests.

Max Parson
Communications
British Columbia Ferry Services Inc

BC FERRIES

REPLY

From: Jackson Snead
To: Max Parson
Sent: Thursday, July 24, 2003
Subject: #20406 Jackson Snead

Dear Max,

Thank you for your reply. I suspected that you may have not received my previous message because I was told that BC Ferries is very accommodating to people with unusual concerns. I can understand that some people would not take this request seriously. I probably wouldn't if I wasn't reminded of it with every breath.

We need to know if it is possible or even necessary to purchase round trip tickets and if we must disembark at the terminals between voyages. I hope not, because we have a skit planned for our entertainment that will climax as the departure whistle blows, but it takes some time to set up the punch line and it would be lost if we have to disembark. We expect at least some of our members to be onboard for 3 and 4 sailings, and we do like our special coffee.

As mentioned, Short Stuff can brew the coffee for us, but we will need an electrical outlet. (We will not repeat the campfire incident.) The final total of our group, (survivors of gastro-effluvium disorder) will be 167 people, 1 seeing eye dog, and one monkey. The animals have the proper tags and papers as certified assistant animals. (The monkey wears a little nurse uniform which is quite cute.

BC FERRIES

He is a male, but he hates trousers.) Just in case you read about our group in the paper last month, I should tell you that we voluntarily banned the pig from large group outings, too unpredictable around a buffet. Rest assured, there will be no assistance pigs onboard at any time.

I hope you are able to answer my questions and if the meeting is as successful as I expect, we may continue as your gracious guests on future voyages

Please respond by e-mail as I have a difficult time speaking these days. I would gladly converse with you by telephone but my variant Tourettes has been acting up and I do not want any misunderstandings.

Thank you,
Jackson

REPLY

From: "Parson, Max D BCF:EX"
To: "'Jackson Snead'"
CC: "Grigore, Ken M BCF:EX"
Subject: #20406 Jackson Snead Jul 24; 3rd e-mail
Date: Friday, July 25, 2003

Hello again, Jackson.

I have forwarded your note to Ken Grigore, Manager, Sales and Reservations. He is handling your requests.

Max Parson
Communications
British Columbia Ferry Services Inc.

BC FERRIES

From: "Grigore, Ken M BCF:EX"
To: "'Jackson Snead'"
Subject: #20406 Jackson Snead Jul 24; 3rd e-mail
Date: Friday, July 25, 2003

Dear Jackson:

This message is in response to your prior emails regarding group travel. You and your group are welcome to travel onboard our vessels. Coffee is available on board most of our vessels at an additional cost. We are not able to allow you to plug in your own coffee maker and brew your own coffee while sailing with us. Depending on the route you choose, we offer various types of flavourful coffee. Unfortunately, you haven't mentioned which route you would like to travel on or the number of adults.

I suggest you click on: http://fcs028/Docs/Applications/Reservations/ to determine which route you and your group would like to sail on. We offer group discounts on many of our sailings. To qualify for a Group Reservation, the group must be comprised of 10 or more fare paying passengers travelling either on foot or in a vehicle licensed to carry 15 or more people (a bus). One person is responsible for payment of the whole group. Reservations can be made up to cut off times depending on Space Availability.

The Group discount applies to groups of 15 OR MORE fare paying passengers reserving a minimum of SEVEN days in advance. These passengers must be travelling together on foot or in a vehicle licensed to carry 15 or more passengers. If you plan on travelling aboard one of our "Spirit," vessels (between Tsawwassen (Vancouver) and Swartz Bay (Victoria), you may consider reserving the Conference Room:

CONFERENCE ROOM: Cost - $60.00 one way or $100.00 return (GST included)

BC FERRIES

- Passengers can be booked for the conference room and must be pre paid.
- this is NON-REFUNDABLE - does NOT include passenger fare
- Reservations are accepted for the conference room onboard the SBC or SVI for use as a private MEETING room.
- Reservations are accepted Mon.-Fri. 08:30 - 15:30 at H.O. Ticketing Office
- Can accommodate up to 20 people.
- Coffee/Tea service is included. No other food service is available to this room.
- Includes TV, VCR, Whiteboard & Overhead Projector.
-To confirm the reservation, a VSA/MAS/AMX must be supplied.

I hope this information is helpful.

REPLY

From: Jackson Snead
To: Max Parson   CC: Grigore, Ken
Sent: Saturday, August 2, 2003
Subject: Thanks for the excellent time

Dear Max and Ken,

On behalf of my group, (Survivors of Gastro-Effluvium Disorder) I would like to pass on our heartfelt appreciation of the hospitality that was shown to us on our recent voyages. As I had previously contacted you with regards to ticketing information and coffee details, I knew that we could expect at least some awareness of our group and our situation from the crew. Our expectations were far surpassed and we were made to feel like normal people from everyone on board.

Our coffee service was excellent, being served

BC FERRIES

piping hot and frequently, and Short Stuff had no difficulty meshing with your obliging crew to fetch it for us. Thank you for not interrupting us and having us disembark at the various terminals as the ship prepared for the return.

As a result, our skit, which culminated with the departure whistle became such a crowd pleaser that we did it every time the vessel departed (4 times in all) and it elicited greater laughs each time. We did have to vary the timing of the acrobatic part of the skit because we had no real knowledge of the time that the whistle would sound, but your announcement was very helpful, and we got the punchline right every time with the help of that.

By the third time I think we set a Guinness record for most people in unison with bodily functions.(166, one of us missed.) I am awaiting their reply and will keep you informed. If awarded, we will give you a plaque to commemorate the event. I must apologize for the way the

Friendly crew members come prepared as best they can.

105

assistance monkey acted though, as I understand he gave one of your stewards a rough time with his ankle. We have spoken to the stewart personally and purchased him several new pairs of socks. The monkey is going for behavior modification at the trainers this week. Thank God we didn't have the pig on board.

This was by far the most successful group meeting we have had, thanks in no small part to the excellent layout of the passenger compartments and the ventilation system. We received very few critical looks from other passengers, except one of the older gentlemen of our group who is partially deaf and unable to regulate himself. (Luckily he is partially blind as well, so he took no notice of the gestures.)We are planning a larger world wide convention of our groups in the spring and will be highly recommending BC Ferries as the place to meet. There could be upwards of 850 Pooters. (That's what we call ourselves, we are not without humor about our condition.)

By the way, if you have someone that you suspect may have this condition, perhaps in your office or social circles, please have them e-mail me and we would be happy to include them into our group. Natural functions are nothing to be ashamed about, and some people just have a little bit more than others. I am sure we will have many more pleasant experiences aboard your vessels in the future.

Toot, toot,
(It still makes me laugh)

Jackson Snead

BC FERRIES

REPLY

From: "Grigore, Ken
To: Jackson Snead
CC: Max Parson
Subject: Re: Thanks for the excellent time

Date: Sunday, August 3 , 2003

Hello Jackson..........I am pleased that you enjoyed your
communication with BC Ferries, it was comic relief for us all in
these busy times. If you can come up with something more creative
and perhaps more imaginative in the future that would be indeed
welcome. But thanks for the (well) entertainment. There is a
wonderful course at U Vic, it's called getting a life 101.

Sent from my BlackBerry Wireless Handheld

GUINNESS BOOK OF RECORDS

A NEW WORLD RECORD

From: Jackson Snead
To: Guinness Book Of Records
Sent: Sunday, August 3, 2003
Subject: A New World Record

Dear Guinness Recording Folk,

I am the representative of Survivors of Gastro Effluvium Disorder and we have a unique situation that may be suitable for your record books.

Just so you know, Gastro Effluvium Disorder causes chronic gas. I acquired mine after having to eat Rhinoceros stew for 10 days in a Kenyan Jail, but every one has their own story. There are currently 167 of us in the lower mainland and Vancouver Island area of British Columbia.

We get together on a regular basis and are currently meeting on the BC Ferries once a month because of their excellent passenger compartment layout and ventilation system. Recently, we had an extended meeting involving a skit which culminated in the punch line coinciding with the blast of the ships departure horn.

We believe we may have set the record for most people in unison with a bodily function.

As we had been crossing the route several times and the punch-line remained the same, (we performed the same skit 4 times as we stayed on board for return sailings) we all got quite good at coordinating our

GUINNESS BOOK OF RECORDS

bodily function at the climax of the punch-line.
(When the ships horn sounded.) We believe we may
have set the record for most people in unison with
a bodily function. As a group we do not get to toot
our own horn very often, so to speak, but we do
know how to toot something, and we can duplicate it
for your cameras if you want.

We would be prepared to stage a demonstration
for you as we do the crossing from Vancouver to
Victoria. BC Ferries has been most cooperative
and obliging with our group. If we coincide the
climax with the ships horn again, it would be a
most tasteful way of letting everyone enjoy a good
bodily function joke.

Do you think we could hold the record for most
people in unison with a bodily function?

Jackson Snead
SGED Rep.

REPLY

From: Customer Relations - Guinness World Records
To: Jackson Snead
Sent: Wednesday, October 1, 2003
Subject: Guinness World Record
Claim ID: 70369
Membership Number: 65698

1 October 2003

Dear Mr. Snead

Thank you for sending us the details of your recent record proposal
for 'Most people in unison with a bodily function'. I am afraid to say
that we are unable to accept this as a Guinness World Record. We

GUINNESS BOOK OF RECORDS

receive over 60,000 enquiries a year from which a small proportion are approved by our experienced researchers to establish new categories. These are not 'made up' to suit an individual proposal, but rather 'evolve' as a result of international competition in a field, which naturally accommodates superlatives of the sort that we are interested in.

We think you will appreciate that we are bound to favor those that reflect the greatest interest.

I appreciate that this may be disappointing to you, but I hope that this does not deter you from trying again. We are always keen to hear from people who wish to set a Guinness World Record. If you should need any advice regarding breaking an existing record or setting a new Guinness World Record please contact us again through our website or directly quoting the above membership number.

Once again thank you for contacting Guinness World Records. We wish you every success with any future record-breaking endeavors.

Yours sincerely,

Sylvia White
Records Research Services

GRANDMA SUSIE@ROUNDUP.COM

MY DILEMMA

From: Jackson Snead
To: Advice @ Grandma Susie.roundup.CBC.ca
Sent: Monday, July 11, 2005
Subject: My Dilemma

Dear Grandma Susie,

I like to use a traditional method of chicken trapping and so I have set up a small trap line inside my chicken coop. I have about 100 chickens and only trap one every two or three days. I don't move the trap around at all and I find that it only traps the stupid ones. Consequently, the remaining chickens are getting smarter and smarter.

In fact, I have several chickens that have been around for about 6 or 7 years and do not even come close to the trap. I have actually seen them holding classes for the little chicks and explaining the trap to them. The problem is that the survivors are getting so smart that they are starting to set traps for me. The other day, when I went to the outhouse, they had somehow got in and weakened the seat so that when I sat down, it gave way and I almost fell through into the pit.

> **The survivors are getting so smart that they are starting to set traps for me.**

I could hear the excited clucking in the henhouse as they waited for my screaming to stop. Luckily, they are not yet as smart as I am, and I was able to free myself without "touching down" as you would

say, but I fear that if they get too smart, one day
I might fall prey to one of their little traps. My
question to you is, do you think that by eating
only the stupid chickens, I will get stupider than
I already am, and that the smart chickens may
actually get an edge on me?
Jackson Snead

REPLY

From: Advice @ Grandma Susie.roundup.CBC.ca
To: Jackson Snead
Sent: Wednesday, July 13, 2005
Subject: My Dilemma

Dear Jackson,

I don't think you can get much stupider, so I wouldn't worry if I were
you.

Grandma Susie

The smartest chickens in the world.

VANCOUVER AQUARIUM

I'D LIKE TO DONATE MY SQUID

From: Jackson Snead
To: Vancouver Aquarium
Sent: Monday, November 28, 2005
Subject: I'd like to Donate My Squid

Dear Vancouver Aquarium,

I am looking to donate Army, my North Atlantic Squid, to your aquarium.

Army has been living with me since I rescued him from a squid jigger in Newfoundland nearly two decades ago while doing a research project on underwater volcanoes.

What caught my attention about the plucky little fellow is that he was born without suckers on his arms. How he survived in the wilds at all is a complete mystery. (We speculate that he only caught really stupid prey) He was about 10 inches long then.

Recently, it has become apparent that Army has outgrown his tank (he is twelve feet from arm-tip to arm-tip now) and has become increasingly ill-tempered. To compensate, I place him in the bathtub where I play with him to calm his nerves. His favorite game is tag.

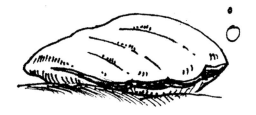

Unfortunately, this has started to become too much of a hardship on us both, and he recently bit off

VANCOUVER AQUARIUM

 one of my fingers during what I thought was a cuddling session.

I would like to send Army to you so that he can live at your aquarium.

He will not attack other fish as long as they don't try to eat him, and he will probably fit in quite well with the other squids at your place.

He looks just like any other Squid, except for the no sucker thing and a skull and crossbones tattoo on his "shoulder" which I gave him while I was on a bit of a bender. (With an eye patch and a tri-pointed hat he looks just like a pirate.)

He eats about 4 lbs of chum per day, (it is best if it is blended to a medium puree) and prefers to be stroked gently while eating.

He also knows a few tricks, (wagon-wheel is his favorite) he likes to arm wrestle and he does a killer impression of Albert Einstein.

I am sure that after an initial adjustment period, Army will become a well loved and popular addition to your facility.

Please let me know if I can ship him to you.

Thanks
Jackson Snead

VANCOUVER AQUARIUM

REPLY

From: Allison Jakes
To: Jackson Snead
Sent: Thursday, December 1, 2005
Subject: Re: I'd like to donate my squid

Hi Jackson,

Thank you for your e-mail. It put a definite smile on my face this morning. We do not usually accept outside specimen donations; however, I have forwarded your e-mail to the Curator for our BC Waters habitats, Ken Daniel. He is the best person to speak with regarding Army.

You may reach Ken by phone at 604 555 3460 or by e-mail at Ken. Daniel@Vancouver Aquarium.

Regards,

Allison Jakes
Development Administrator
Vancouver Aquarium Marine Science Centre
PO Box 3232
Vancouver, BC, V6B 3X8
Tel: (604) 555 - 3509
Fax: (604) 555-6593
Visit the Aquarium Website www.vanaqua.org

Check out the Salmonchanted Evening Website
www.salmonchantedevening.org

Canadian Charitable Tax Number: 11928 2119 RR0001
US Charitable Tax Number: 98-0050185

VANCOUVER AQUARIUM

From: Ken Daniel
To: Jackson Snead
Sent: Tuesday, December 6, 2005
Subject: I'd Like to donate My Squid

Dear Jackson,

Thank you for the offer to donate your squid Army. He really sounds like an amazing critter. Unfortunately before we would ever be able to take him as a donation we would like it if you could email us a photo of him?

Thanks again for your inquiry.

Cheers,
Ken

Ken Daniel
Curator of B.C. Waters
Vancouver Aquarium
Marine Science Centre
(604) 555-3474

REPLY

From: Jackson Snead
To: Ken Daniel, Vancouver Aquarium
Sent: Tuesday, December 6, 2005
Subject: Photo of Army

Dear Ken,

Here is the photo of Army as requested. I was able to catch him at a rare moment when he is out of his tank and doing his Albert Einstein imitation. Its an uncanny likeness isn't it? It took a lot to teach him that. (He kept doing Sidney Poitier.)

116

VANCOUVER AQUARIUM

Army likes to do impressions of famous geniuses.

I will be very sad to see him go, but I know he will have a better life at your facility. He will probably make lots of new friends and I can always get another (smaller) squid in Chinatown. Would it be possible to visit him in your facility once he is settled in? I would like to swim with him again like we used to in the good old days.

I will enclose some of his prized possessions with him when I send him, like his pirate hat and tuxedo. (He only wears the tux on New years and does he look sharp!) It would be best if you keep these items near his tank so he can see them. I think it's a comfort to him. The drycleaner once lost his Armani Suit and he was upset for weeks.

It is a mixed blessing that he is going though, shortly after this photo he squirted ink and hit my dog, Spot. Luckily Spot is a Dalmatian so it doesn't much matter. Please let me know when I can send him. I think

117

VANCOUVER AQUARIUM

there is a seat sale on with Greyhound soon so if
we can hit that, I would very much appreciate it.
If you have trouble with this picture, please let
me know. I sent it as the attachment too.

Thanks,
Jackson

REPLY

From: Jackson Snead
To: Ken Daniel, Vancouver Aquarium
Sent: Tuesday, December 13, 2005
Subject: Destiny Calls

Dear Ken,

Last week I sent you a photo of Army doing an
Albert Einstein impression with the hopes of
getting him adopted into your aquarium for his
twilight years. Your kind offer to take care of him
has touched us deeply and we very much appreciate
it. However, since then, we were contacted by

Seaworld of the Netherlands
who hope to use his unique
talents in their production
of "Squid of La Mancha" to be
staged off-off Broadway as
they say.

Apparently, he will get top
billing and has a special
segment during intermission
to perform his imitations.
We have decided to accept
their offer, which comes with
more chum than Army has ever

118

imagined. He will now be going by his new name of "Squiddy, the Amazing".

I hope that Army will enjoy his new life as a star performer touring various theatrical venues and expanding his repertoire. I expect he is glad to be out on the road again and free to seek his fortunes. He always was a plucky little fellow.

They expect to be in Vancouver sometime this spring and I can get you tickets for this event if you like. (Please limit it to eight people and pets.) I hope you are not too disappointed with this little twist, however, I assure you, that Army would love to meet you and give you a hug after your kind offer last week.

Thanks for your kindness, and I will pass on wishes from you to Army, to "break a leg."

Thanks,
Jackson

BUFFALO ENSEMBLE THEATRE

BOOKING YOUR THEATRE

From: Jackson Snead
To: Buffalo Ensemble Theatre
Sent: Thursday, December 23, 2005
Subject: Booking Your Theatre

Dear Sirs,

I would like to book our production of "Squid of La Mancha" into your theatre for some time in 2007.

It is a showstopper of a production utilizing sea creatures to recreate the timeless classic stage show.

We have large thin vertical aquariums where the sea creatures perform. They swim and wave to the music in conjunction with bubbles and colored lights. The songs are performed by parrots and Cockatoos except for the aria, "Buy me a Wanderer" which is sung by Annabelle Solstice. The show stars Squiddy the Amazing. We have been selling out all across the Netherlands and expect to take America by storm. (You may have seen an excerpt on CNN last week.)

It is a showstopper of a production utilizing sea creatures to recreate the timeless classic stage show.

Can you answer a few questions for me before we book our production to your theatre, such as;

Are there any applicable laws regarding using sea creatures or birds in our production which would prevent us from performing in your area?

Is there a reliable supplier of chum in your area?

BUFFALO ENSEMBLE THEATRE

(Must be dolphin friendly.)

Can you let me know which dates are available in early 2007? Can you provide a smoke machine with #104 Sancel odorless pink morning style mist?

Please get back to me soon so that we are able to plan accordingly.

Thanks,
Jackson Snead
Production manager,
Sea Stars Theatre Group

REPLY

From: Buffalo Ensemble Theatre
To: Jackson Snead
Sent: Saturday, December 31, 2005
Subject: RE: Booking Your Theatre

Jackson,

Thanks for this inquiry. Our theatre company is located in a school, so unfortunately we are unable to provide a space for this production.

You have a strikingly original concept, and we look forward to seeing this show when you do find a location in Western New York.

Best wishes,

Rupert Handy
Buffalo Ensemble Theatre

121

ISLAND WINDOWS

WE NEED SPECIAL WINDOWS

From: Jackson Snead
To: Island Windows
Sent: Friday, October 21, 2005
Subject: We Need Special Windows

Dear Island Windows

We are currently designing a luxury home for Harold Balbag, heir to the Balbag Ant Farm fortune in North Saanich. There are about 45 windows throughout the house and your company has come very well recommended. Normally we would deal directly with a salesman, however, there are a couple of eccentricities that Mr. Balbag has asked us to inquire about.

Since he is quite fond of ant farms, having made millions of dollars from them, he has required

He has required that the space between the glass be filled with sand and ants.

that the space between the glass be filled with sand and ants, thus giving him an ant farm in each window. They should be at least half filled with white silicone sand, # 190, except one, which will house the ashes of Margaret Balbag, Harold's beloved wife.

Can you also manufacture a hole about 1 inch in diameter near the top of each inside pane through which food can be dropped?

He will find a cork himself to fill the hole and keep the ants inside. He is prepared to pay a

122

ISLAND WINDOWS

premium for this service and he will be forever indebted to you if this can be accomplished.

Please let us know soon as he needs to prepare for the cremation of his wife and the ashes to be forwarded to you for the installation. We can supply the ants.

Thanks,
Jackson Snead

REPLY

From: Frank Richards
To: Jackson Snead
Sent: Friday, October 21, 2005
Subject: Re: Island Windows web site feedback

Thanks for your enquiry. It's not a problem for us to meet those specifications, in fact, that is exactly how we build windows every day here at Island Windows. We'll be in touch with you soon to arrange an estimate.

Thanks for thinking of us.

Pi55 BEER

WELCOME TO THE PISS BEER WEBSITE

TWO GREAT NEW OFFERS FROM THE Pi55 BEER CO.

The "PISS PAK"

"Piss Pak"

Now you can enjoy the great taste of Piss and Piss Weak regardless of where you live. The Piss Pak was developed in response to the massive demand we have received both in Australia and overseas for these distinctive brands, and we now offer delivery to your door anywhere in the world. Presented in a stylish gift box, the Piss Pak contains a T-shirt, a stubby holder and one bottle each of Piss and PissWeak.

Click on the pic for pricing info

Be the envy of your friends or impress them with your original gift giving ideas. Order your Piss Pak today and discover why Australians love their Piss!

Slab O` Piss Home Delivery

A very special offer for Australians who have heard of the legendary aussie brew but have not yet had the chance to try it. Thanks to an unbeatable freight deal, Piss and Piss Weak can now be delivered straight to your door almost anywhere in **Australia***. Be the hit of your next backyard barbecue or delight friends when you arrive for dinner with your very own supply of icy cold Piss. Cut out the middleman and order your slab of Piss today. *Offer extends to Australian residents only. Where duty is levied...

Click on the pic for pricing info

To find out more about these distinctive beers click on the Pisstory link. Direct sales are available from local stockists listed on the links below.

OZ Bottleshop or UK Bottleshop

124

Pi55 BEER

FOUNTAIN OF YOUTH

From: Jackson Snead
To: drinkin@pi55.com
Sent: Friday, June 16, 2006 5:39 AM
Subject: Fountain of Youth

Dear Piss Beer Meisters,

Last week a friend brought some of your beer back from Australia and I got to try it for the first time. It was really good. I had about four and then got up to go to the bathroom when I noticed I had become slightly aroused. Not out of control, but you know, just slightly. So I had a couple more and these feelings kept increasing.

I don't know what you put in your beer, but like I said, it makes me all suave and virile and a real studly kind of guy. I think it even makes me smarter.

Now, I should tell you that I am an experienced 45 year old beer drinker and not some teenager with raging hormones. After about 8 beer in total I went home and enjoyed some marital bliss with my wife.

It was amazing. It was like being 20 yrs old again.

I have not felt that potent in years. The wife also agreed that I was much more debonair and exciting then usual and that if that's what that beer does for me I should drink it all the time. She thought I had turned into some kind of James Bond type character. (She kept calling me Roger)

Pi55 BEER

I tried to duplicate the effect with domestic beer from Canada here, but all I got was uncoordinated and sloppy and the wife finds me terribly unattractive when that happens. I don't know what you put in your beer, but like I said, it makes me all suave and virile and a real studdly kind of guy. I think it even makes me smarter.

Can you tell me if you put something special in the beer? If you do, you should market it for its virile effects. I'll bet it would knock Viagra right off the market. Who wouldn't want a beer that gets you ready to love-rumble?

Anyway, I was also wondering if you guys are going to start selling your beer in Canada soon? I'd be willing to testify for its miraculous effects. You could do a commercial that showed a before and after of me and the wife.

She'd gladly serve me a case or two of your beer. Then you would get to see how happy she gets and how much better looking and suave I am when I'm plastered on your beer. Please get back to me quickly as I hope to "get me some" again real soon.

Thanks
Jackson Snead

PS. Does this happen to everyone who drinks your beer

Pi55 BEER

REPLY

From: The Great Britain
To: Jackson Snead
Sent: Monday, July 03, 2006 6:32 PM
Subject: Re: Fountain of Youth

Hi Jackson,

Thanks for your highly entertaining email! While I can make no claim to be knowingly responsible for your enhanced swarthiness while under the influence of our product, you can rest assured I will be letting everyone over here know that it has had this effect!

No luck at this stage though in finding a distributor in Canada.

Regards,
Craig

REPLY

From: Jackson Snead
To: The Great Britain
Sent: Friday, July 07, 2006 10:01 AM
Subject: Re: Fountain of Youth

Dear Craig,

Thanks for your quick reply to my e-mail. To bad you don?t have a Canadian Distributor, but I'm sure you probably do just fine "Down Under". I know I am, for now anyway. I just thought I'd update you on the most recent development with your beer. A bunch of us boys were changing after doing a rehearsal scuba dive for the underwater premier performance of "Squid Of La Mancha" and we, (really it was Carl and we think he might be bent like a

Pi55 BEER

curly-fry if you know what I mean) noticed that
some guys had major shrinkage and other guys (me
included) had no shrinkage at all.

The defining factor was what beer we had for
breakfast. Yours, of course, proved to be the
better. After the locker room comparison, those
baby-carrot-boys, as we now call them, can't even
look me in the eye. Bert even started to stutter.
So now I have a few of your beers packed away for
the next dive cause I kind of like being Big Man On
Campus, if you know what I mean.

If I were you guys, I'd put right on your label
that your beer reverses the shrinkage factor. It
should really help to sell it to the beach crowd.

Jackson

REPLY

From: The Great Britain
To: Jackson Snead
Sent: Thursday, July 06, 2006 7:10 PM
Subject: Re: Fountain of Youth

Thanks Jackson,

Obviously seems it's the right brew for you but I reckon they'd create
a department of improper claims just to shoot me down if I tried to go
public with your good news story. Keep up the good work,

Craig.

Pi55 BEER

From: Albert Swinehinderson
To: The Great Britain
Sent: Saturday, July 08, 2006 6:04 PM
Subject: Just a quick question

Hello Craig,

My friend Jackson Snead told me of your beer and I am requesting your help. I need to save the world and can only do so by swimming naked across half a mile of open ocean behind my arch rival, Harry Longfellow, to an island where I am to meet a crazy shaman who will then release wild dogs which will attack and eat the man with the smallest penis. It is imperative that I survive and defeat Harry Longfellow. Do you know of any substance that may reduce the miniaturization of my manhood by freezing water? Any assistance you can render regarding this matter would be most appreciated.

Thank You,
Albert Swinehinderson

REPLY

From: The Great Britain
To: Albert Swinehinderson
Sent: Sunday, July 09, 2006 8:03 PM
Subject: Re: Just a quick question

Hi Albert,

In Australia we would say you are taking the piss - very funny but not to be believed. Keep up the good work!

Craig

M&M MEATS

WE NEED SPECIALTY MEATS

From: Jackson Snead
To: M&M Meats
Sent: Saturday, November 5, 2005
Subject: We Need Specialty Meats

Dear M&M Meats

For the last 15 years I have traveled the globe as an independent interpreter and spent my spare time pursuing a hobby of searching for the worlds most delicious foods.

Although I hate to give up my wandering ways, changing world politics and a spotty driving record have caused me to settle down in Victoria, BC. I plan to open one of the world's only indigenous people's restaurants, "Eskimo Elli's". I will specialize in the foods of first nation's people from all around the world. I am featuring the most delicious dishes that I have found in my travels. Coconut cream   fish cakes from Fiji, Australian Roo tail soup, Indonesian monkey finger sandwiches, Eskimo Mukmuk Pie, and Paraguayan Penguin Puffs are all on the menu.

Cockatoo-yas.................................
Cod Wallops.............................$22.50
Lizard Links.........................$3.25
................................$6.75

I have since been informed that your company is one of the foremost suppliers of meat in North

130

M&M MEATS

ESKIMO ELLI'S RESTAURANT

Squirrel Nut Pudding......................$2.50
Kangaroonies......................$4.25
Seal Face Pie......................$5.50
Tiger Titties......................$12.00

America and that you would be the most likely to be able to help me. I am opening in the spring of 2006 and am hoping to secure suppliers for the wide variety of meats that I will need.I need approximately 500 lbs of Walrus loin in the first month, (May) growing to 1500lbs a month by the end of the summer. I expect to go through about 1000 Elkhorn Penguins during my Penguin-on-a-Stick promotion in early June, and probably, if I can get the right recipe, will need a barrel of southern red tailed sidewinder hoop snakes for Snakesicle September. (Like Popsicles, but with snakes, delicious.)

I presently have a New Guinea Grub supplier, but I would be interested if you can get me a more secure or alternate source. I cannot afford to put all my grubs in one basket, so to speak.

I would also be interested in sharing some of the wonderful recipes with you so that you could put them on your web page. I have a great one for Walrus Wuskers, they are so juicy. I am sure that this will help grow the market for a wide variety of meats and make it worth your while to import them.Please let me know if you can help me, I would like to get the menu finalized by Christmas.

Thanks,
Jackson Snead

M&M MEATS

REPLY

From: "Melody Weiss"
To: Jackson Snead
Sent: Monday, November 7, 2005
Subject: RE: mmmeatshops.com feedback

Good morning Mr. Snead,

Panda Patties.................................
Walrus Wuskers.............................$8.50
Goat Grunts...................................$15.25
Penguin Puffs................................$10.75
.......$7.50

Thank you for your email concerning Walrus loins. We currently work with 80 suppliers. The products arrive to our warehouse ready for sale to our customers. We do not sell any "raw" materials.

Thank you for your interest in working with M&M Meat Shops Ltd. Good luck in your new venture.

Melody Weiss
Assistant Buyer
M&M Meat Shops Ltd.

REPLY

From: Jackson Snead
To: Melody Weiss
Sent: Tuesday, November 8, 2005
Subject: Re: mmmeatshops.com feedback

Dear Melanie,

Thanks for getting back to me so quickly. This is very exciting news. I had no idea there were so many walrus loin suppliers.

M & M MEATS

I would be happy to order products that are ready
for sale and already prepared, that will make the
health inspectors happier too. They were really not
fond of the whole do it yourself onsite butcher
shop so it was under review anyway. I'll bet with
that many suppliers you have a whole variety of
walrus delicacies that I have never even heard of
before.

Do you have some stuffed with cheese? If possible,
I would like to stick to either free range walrus
or wild, no factory farmed product please. (People
say it doesn't affect the taste, but I can tell.)

Please send me a list of your walrus items and if
possible, a list of other pinniped products.I am
very excited about this.

Jackson Snead

ESKIMO ELLI'S RESTAURANT

Vegetarian Menu

Grass 'n Dirt...$5.25

Sticks 'n Stones...$11.50

Hunk-0-Sod...$8.75

Puddle Pudding..$2.50

M & M MEATS

REPLY

From: Melody Weiss
To: Jackson Snead
Sent: Wednesday, November 9, 2005
Subject: RE: mmmeatshops.com feedback

Please accept my apologies. I have mislead you with my last email.

We do not have any of the products available that you are looking for either in raw material or finished goods.

Please feel free to review our products on our website www. mmmeatshops.com.

Melody Weiss
Assistant Buyer
M&M Meat Shops Ltd.

REPLY

From: Jackson Snead
To: Melody Weiss
Sent: Thursday, November 10
Subject: Re: mmmeatshops.com feedback
Dear Melody,

How about penguins? Got any penguins?

Jackson

ESKIMO LLI'S RESTAURANT

DESSERT MENU

Clam Brulée................................$8.00
Salmon Squeezings....................$12.50
Chum Glacée...............................$9.75
Otter Chocolate..........................$11.00

DR. MAGIC BOX

TEST MY POTATO

I have changed the name of this group to make my life simpler, but be careful. They are out there in a variety of diguises...

I came across Dr. Magic Box at a display booth where several of their members were diagnosing people who had been wired to their device. Upon reading their brochure and speaking to them, they claim that their device can reveal many hidden imbalances and illness within the body and at the same time, correct the energy imbalances that cause the sickness.

They also claim to be able to do subspace diagnosis, where healings can be performed on people or pets not even attached to the device. Personally, I found their claims a bit wacky so I decided to see if I could get them to test a potato for me and see if it had different readings then a human.

Their device sells for about $14,000.00 and practitioners charge up to $100.00 per hour to hook you up to their units.

The following material is taken directly from their website, so that you may judge for yourself.

How does the Magic Box work?
The Magic Box is a highly sophisticated program with sensors attached by wires to the ankles, wrists and forehead that measure and feed resonance information between the Magic Box and the client. The ionic exchanges of reaction that take place in your body and brain (at 1/100 of a second) are measured as energetic components in your body.

With a feedback loop, the device measures your resonance pulse and sends back an alternate pulse to which your body responds. In turn, your body alters its own reactance pulse, thus creating a change.

DR. MAGIC BOX

For example, from pain to no pain, malignant to benign, compulsive to anxiety-free, imbalance to balance. Due to the 'autofocus' function, the Magic Box can adjust bio-feedback therapies to ensure and constantly adjust the correct settings during therapy.

The Magic Box is an Evoked Potential Bio-Feedback Device. This function eliminates the need for expert knowledge about rife, bio-com and electro-acupuncture.

The Magic Box has nearly 10,000 items in the test matrix! What does the Magic Box actually do?
The Magic Box scans the client's body like a virus-scan on a computer, looking for everything from viruses, deficiencies, weaknesses, allergies, abnormalities and food sensitivities.

How does the Magic Box try to revitalize the body?
As the Magic Box has been devised using the principles of Quantum Physics, that question is easier asked than answered.

Can you use the Magic Box on animals/pets?
YES.

'Subspace' Operation
The Magic Box has a built-in facility which allows it to perform even without the harness. This radionic equivalent mode enables distant testing and therapy. .

What is the retail price of the complete Magic Box System?
The device currently retails for $14,000. USD

DR. MAGIC BOX

From: Jackson Snead
To: Dr. Magic Box
Sent: Monday, October 31, 2005
Subject: Test My Potato

Dear Sirs,

Recently my Grandfather, (we called him Mufpah) passed away and I inherited his Magic Box. My grandfather took extensive notes while using his machine, and he developed a method for increasing the yield of his potato patch through its use.

Recently, I started to duplicate his experiments and I had some very interesting readings. While doing a

I figure if Muftah wants to dress up a potato, carry it in her pocket and talk to it like her dead husband, what's the harm?

measurement and checking the data on one of the potatoes, it had very unusual readings which completely duplicated the readings of the last time Mufpah measured himself!

It is a complete anomaly which stands out from the other potatoes that I measured. Muftah (Grandma) says it is Mufpah reincarnated into a potato and she refuses to eat it. I have no explanation for it, but remain open minded. I figure if Muftah wants to dress up a potato, carry it in her pocket and talk to it like her dead husband, what's the harm? Unfortunately my siblings do not feel the same way, and are insisting that we take Mufpah potato for further tests.

This is where you come in. Can I send you the

DR. MAGIC BOX

potato and can you run some tests to see if it does indeed have a similar response to a human? This would set Muftah's mind at ease and she will then know whether to proceed with renewing her wedding vows or make a potato salad. I do appreciate your help on this matter, and I think you are the only people that can help me.If you can do this I will courier Mufpah potato to you, along with your fee, and tell Muftah that Mufpah is away on business. You will have to return him by courier quickly though, as she is likely to become suspicious. Mufpah had a girlfriend once and she has never forgotten.

Please let me know how much it will cost. Thank you for your help in advance.

Jackson Snead

From: Jackson Snead
To: Dr. Magic Box
Sent: Wednesday, November 2, 2005
Subject: Did you get my e-mail?

Dear Dr. Magic Box,

I know it has only been a few days since I wrote to you asking for help, but I just want to know if you got my e-mail. Please get back to me soon, Muftah is driving me crazy and I have to do something soon. If you did not get it, just let me know and I will sent it again.

Thanks,
Jackson Snead

DR. MAGIC BOX

REPLY

From: Dr. Magic Box
To: Jackson Snead
Sent: Wednesday, November 2, 2005
Subject: Re: Did you get my e-mail?

Hi There .We have been very busy .

Please give me a call 6504-2319-2334.You have to admit that on first read it could be taken as a interesting story .

If you are in need of help we will all help.

Stev Bernard.

REPLY

From: Jackson Snead
To: Dr. Magic Box
Sent: Thursday, November 3, 2005
Subject: Test My Potato

Dear Stev

Thanks for getting back to me so quickly. I am so glad you will help us out and test our potato.

Muftah (Grandma) has agreed to let you test it, so take a few days if you want.

I do understand upon re-reading the letter how you can think it was a bit nutty. It was written in a highly emotional state and it doesn't begin to scratch the surface of our family dynamics, which I am sure you do not want to delve into.

DR. MAGIC BOX

Anyhow, I would have got back to you earlier today, but with the wind, the power went out and a tree fell on Romeo and Juliet's dog house, trapping their puppies, (Woofbah, Woofcah and Woofdah. They're OK and so cute!)I tried to have a friend call you at the number provided, but it reached some Chinese Food Store in San Francisco.

You may want to check the number you gave me.

Regardless, I should tell you that I am deaf, which is why Mufpah originally purchased your machine. Unfortunately, he made some modifications to the machine in a misguided attempt to improve it, which is how it got adapted to the potato patch. For the test can you simply hook up the potato in question to your machine and see if you can determine if there is a reincarnated soul in it? All I need

Unfortunately, he made some modifications to the machine in a misguided attempt to improve it, which is how it got adapted to the potato patch.

is a third party to verify my suspicions and then Muftah will realize that she should let go and start the healing process.

I am going fishing for a couple of weeks at first light tomorrow, but I have left instructions for Junior, (my brother) to send you the potato as soon as we know where to send it. I will place $100.00 cash inside the package to cover fees and return courier. I hope that is enough.

If not, just tell me what you need and Junior (We

140

call him Puftah) will add it to the package. If
there is any change, just send it back with the
potato. (I refuse to call it Mufpah.)

Thanks
Jackson Snead

REPLY

From: Dr. Magic Box
To: Jackson Snead
Sent: Thursday, November 3, 2005
Subject: Re: Test My Potato

Hi There. Our number is 1-604-555-2334/1-604-555-4624

Where are you calling from? Leave me your number so I can call you

Steve Bernard

REPLY

From: Jackson Snead
To: Dr. Magic Box
Sent: Friday, November 4, 2005
Subject: Test My Potato

Hi Steve,

We live on Mudge Island just off Nanaimo and there
is no phone service, plus as mentioned previously,
I am deaf. I have to travel to Nanaimo to use an
Internet Cafe.

Please get back soon with an address to send off
the potato because Junior will be rowing over to
check the e-mails later today and send off the

potato. I don't care where we send it or to who, I am sure there are many qualified practitioners in the area, or we can send it to Vancouver.

We don't want to have Junior row back to the island with the potato and then have to get Muftah to let him take it away again. Believe me, it was hard enough to convince her to let him take it the first time.

> *We don't want to have Junior row back to the island with the potato and then have to get Muftah to let him take it away again. Believe me, it was hard enough to convince her to let him take it the first time.*

All we need is a test for a reincarnated soul in the potato. I am sure you can do it, and I hope the payment is sufficient. I am leaving now for a fishing trip up the coast and I hope we have been able to accomplish our goal by the time I get back.

I really appreciate your help in this matter, I know it sounds wacky, but Muftah is kind of wacky and she makes us all wacky when she gets weird.

Thanks,
Jackson

DR. MAGIC BOX

Potatoes have feelings too, you know.

DR. MAGIC BOX

From: Dr. Magic Box
To: Jackson Snead
Sent: Friday, November 4, 2005
Subject: Test My Potato

Now I am skeptical. Someone can call me and spaek to me live

Steve

SEX SHOP CANADA

BENJAMIN BUNNY NEEDS A SEX TOY

From: Jackson Snead
To: Sex Shop Canada
Sent: Monday, September 26, 2005
Subject: Benjamin Bunny needs a sex toy

Dear Sex Shop Canada

I have been an animal breeder and sex toy user for many years and I hope you can help me out. I am the proud owner of Benjamin Braithwaite Bunny the 33rd.

He is a champion Mini-Rex stud rabbit and responsible for the entire western wing of the prized Alsa-Bonnard bloodlines. He is very well house trained, and we enjoy living in the same space, as you can see by the photo, but he does have a problem.

He humps anything that moves, literally. Everything you have heard about horny rabbits is true. You can't take two steps without him jumping on your foot. If you wiggle your arm, he grabs on to your forearm like green on a frog. If I have a guest over, and they get a little too relaxed on the couch, he's humping their face. He's hard to get off too; he has big claws and is very determined. And believe me, if he gets a good grip on your ears, its best if you just pucker up and close your eyes. It's really hard on the social life.

So I was wondering, could you people make a special love doll for Benjamin? I would suggest something that looks like a rabbit, perhaps with a vibrating "special Part". As far as he is concerned, I don't think he really cares what it looks like. It could

SEX SHOP CANADA

Benjamin likes to prepare with a good breakfast.

be a troll doll with a bag on its head as long as
it gave a shake or a twitch once in a while. For
your manufacturing purposes, Benjamin is about 4
lbs and about the size of a medium size chicken
like you would buy at Safeway. I think his wiener,
(when erect) is about 1 ½ inches long and seems to
be about 3/8 of an inch in diameter, but admittedly
it is a bit blurry when I see it. (It's either too
close or moving too fast to get a good look at) The
love doll should also collect and store his bunny
juice since I do sell it to other breeders.

It would probably need some kind of vacuum suction
thing that drew it into a special receptacle,

which could be easily removed. I think he would appreciate some kind of self-lubricating device too. (Pump action should work fine.) I would be willing to replenish a reservoir once in a while.

I know this is an unusual request, but it could open up a completely new market for you and it will sure make my life easier. Please get back to me soon and give me some idea of the cost. Until I get this love doll, I will have to continue to tape my ears back.

Jackson Snead

REPLY

From: Sex Shop Canada
To: Jackson Snead
Sent: Wednesday, September 28, 2005
Subject: Re: Product Inquiry or Request

Hello. Thank you for your email. We aren't aware of any toys made for pets on the market, so there isn't anything I could really recommend. Theoretically speaking, since a doll would not have the scent of a live rabbit or act like a rabbit, I don't know if a live rabbit would take to it regularily, in the same way that a human would regularily choose to use a toy.

If you would like, we can forward your email to our suppliers and manufacturers, and see what they have to say. I can't promise that they will respond to us or to you directly, but we can certainly try. Please confirm if we have permission to forward your details to the appropriate companies.

Kind regards,

Teri

SEX SHOP CANADA

REPLY

From: Jackson Snead
To: Sex Shop Canada
Sent: Friday, September 30,2005
Subject: Benjamin Bunny Needs a sex toy

Hi Teri,

Thanks for your quick reply. We don't need to worry about it smelling like a rabbit to entice Benjamin, believe me, it's going to smell like a rabbit pretty darn soon after he gets a hold of it. Benjamin will hump anything including Grandma and the Christmas turkey. Who would have thought that a rabbit could leap from the table onto a moving target like Grandma's head? And who would have thought that Grandma was wearing a wig? So this Christmas, he's staying in his cage until dinner is cleared and everyone has gone home. Grandma says if he comes near her again, she's going to f**** him up. And I am using nice words compared to her. I guess it was an expensive wig and she was upset that nobody would eat the turkey stuffing.

Who would have thought that a rabbit could leap from the table onto a moving target like Grandma's head?

By all means ask around and see if there is anyone else who can help me. I am also aware of a walrus breeder in Nunavut who needs help.

Jackson Snead

SEX SHOP CANADA

REPLY

From: Sex Shop Canada
To: Jackson Snead
Sent: Wednesday, October 5, 2005
Subject: Benjamin Bunny Needs A Sex Toy

Dear Jackson

Hello. Thanks for your email. We received the photos and email.
As we mentioned, I can't promise that they will respond to us at all.
As a retailer only, we're not able to extract a quick response from
various manufacturers. We can only forward inquiries, but we may
never receive a response.

Since the concept of toys for animals is more or less unprecedented
as far as I know, I don't imagine that any quick solution will be
coming from any manufacturer. For a faster solution, I can only
suggest you try some sort of home-made solution.

Kind regards, Teri

REPLY

From: Jackson Snead
To: Sex Shop Canada
Sent: Wednesday, October 5, 2005
Subject: Benjamin Bunny Needs A Sex Toy

Dear Teri,

Thanks for keeping me informed of your progress. I
realize that there may not be many companies that
can help me, so I have decided to take your advice.
I have some experience in breeding animals and I
may just be the one to "fill a niche", so to speak.

149

SEX SHOP CANADA

Over the years, I have bred dogs, cats, rabbits, beavers, pygmy goats, horses, chickens, pandas bears, walrus, moose, and snakes. I even had a hand in developing a cross between a wolverine and a squirrel, (it was a voracious nut-eater.)

Many of my methods have been adopted by other breeders and are credited with maintaining the populations of some endangered species i.e.; the Sullivan's leaf snail. In my experience, the love doll only has to barely resemble the female of the species. In fact, for the walrus, all we used was a rolled up shag carpet and later, even though it still smelled like "The Far North", we just duct taped on a couple of antlers for the moose.

Anyway, we are trying to make it a little better for the critters, which is where you come in. Could you find or create for us a series of "special parts" in various sizes? We need; little finger size, middle finger size, thumb size and shoulder deep size. (That's for the elephant.) My current surrogate for Benjamin (a towel) lacks any special attachments and relies purely on his own frustration and friction.

While he does not seem to mind, larger animals do tend to loose interest quickly and several of my colleague's more finicky animals have gone on to "have their way with" their owners. (I learned that lesson early and I don't turn my back on them anymore.)

Thanks,
Jackson

SEX SHOP CANADA

REPLY

From: Sex Shop Canada
To: Jackson Snead
Sent: Friday, October 7, 2005
Subject: Benjamin Bunny Needs A Sex Toy

Hello. Thank you for your email. Since we are a retailer only, we're not able to manufacture anything direct to customers. We don't have the capability to order custom parts. We can forward this email to other manufacturers, but we have not yet received a response to previous emails. This does sound like a large task and my best recommendation is that you approach a plastics manufacturer who could create and mold the sleeves. We will let you know if anyone responds to us regarding this and previous emails. Sorry if we can't be of more help, this just isn't within our capabilities.

Kind regards,

Teri

From: Sex Shop Canada
To: Jackson Snead
Sent: Friday, October 7, 2005
Subject: Fwd: Re: Benjamin Bunny Needs A Sex Toy

Hello. I have just been advised that another possibility is to contact BMS Enterprises. We don't have any business relations with them, so we don't have any contact info. Look them up in the phonebook or visit their retail website www.arentwenaughty.com and ask to be directed to their BMS Enterprises division. Best of luck!

Kind regards,
Teri

151

SEX SHOP CANADA

THE STORE FOR COUPLES AT PLAY

Shop By Category

Hot New Items
Bestsellers
For Couples
For Women
For Men
Lingerie
Novelties & Lotions
Books & Videos
Specialty Items
Sale Items

XML SUBSCRIBE

Estimate Price in:
US Dollars
[Update]

FREE SHIPPING
click for more info

Discreet Packaging

NOVELTIES AND LOTIONS

19 Products for this category | 7 Products Displayed.

<< Previous | 1 | 2 | Next >>

7 inch Wild Willies - Freddy Bear

$11.95 ($9.46 USD)

7 inch Wild Willies - Mammoth Moose

$11.95 ($9.46 USD)

7 inch Wild Willie - Pink Rabbit

$11.95 ($9.46 USD)

7 inch Wild Willie - Blue Rabbit

$11.95 ($9.46 USD)

7 inch Wild Willie - Purple Rabbit

$11.95 ($9.46 USD)

7 inch Wild Willie - Purple Rabbit

$11.95 ($9.46 USD)

Wild Willie Boys with Clip Chain

$5.95 ($4.30 USD)

TIM HORTON'S

COFFEE CUP CONSERVATION

From: Jackson Snead
To: Tim Horton's Donuts
Sent: Monday, July 11, 2005
Subject: Coffee Cup Conservation

Dear Tim Horton's,

I, like many other consumers am alarmed at the amount of stuff it takes to just have a cup of coffee these days. If I have a take-out coffee,

I have the cup, a cardboard heat protection band around it, a little sugar packet, one or two little plastic cream cups, a stir stick, the removable top of the cup and a napkin.

We at Bean Counters International Corporation did a little study to determine the amount of energy required to actually brew and serve a cup of take-out coffee.

We counted all the components, from the coffee farming and preparation of the beans, the oil production for the plastic, the farming and harvesting of the trees, sugar and cream and the manufacturing of the paper products and stir sticks.

We calculate that the amount of energy consumed for one cup of coffee could power a toaster for 400 days continually, play a 45 rpm record at loud (60 decibels) volume for 98 days or power a Mercedes Benz from Edmonton to Calgary with two passengers. (based on a 560 SL convertible with the top down.)

Conversely, it would take a hamster, (or hamsters)

153

TIM HORTON'S

19,000 days of continual wheel running to generate the same amount of power. (Based on a 6 inch Hartz hamster wheel hooked up to a Mark 5 Grundig Teeny-Tiny Turbine.)

And that is for just one cup of coffee. When you calculate all the energy multiplied by the many cups of coffee served per day, we could go to the sun and back in a 4 cylinder Honda Civic.

Like you, I was amazed, but I decided to do something about it.As a result, we have introduced the Coffee Conservation Center.

This is a little unit that sits next to the cream and sugar station in a coffee shop and recycles the used materials.

Instead of throwing out the paper cups, they are wiped, sterilized (almost) and put back into circulation for the next customer.

Chain-wide, your company would save about 16 billion dollars per year and save enough energy worldwide to put a colony of dogs on Mars...

The excess coffee that is not consumed is poured into one of four reservoirs; (black, creamed, cream and sugar or black-sugar) and then filtered and warmed with a small fire fueled by the used napkins, (only the ones that can't be flattened and put back into circulation), the stir sticks are cleaned with the cups or burned if they are worn out.

If our unit is adopted by all your stores, we estimate that this method of conservation would save 180 acres of rain forest per month and reduce your costs by a staggering $4657.00 per month per store.

Chain-wide, your company would save about 16 billion dollars per year and save enough energy worldwide to put a colony of dogs on Mars and sustain them for 8 days. (This does not include the return trip though.) Our little unit is currently being certified and will be ready to be installed in your stores shortly.

Can I count on your corporation to order a few units and help save the planet?

Jackson Snead
Marketing Manager
Bean Counters International Corp.,
Conservation Unit,

REPLY

From: Tim Horton's Donuts
To: Jackson Snead
Sent: Wednesday, July 13, 2005
Subject: Re: Coffee Cup Conservation

Dear Snead,

I would like to thank you for writing to us at our Head Office in Oakville. At Tim Hortons we pride ourselves on our quality service and product. We appreciate the time you have taken to offer us your services.

Mr. Snead, as I am sure you can imagine we get numerous suggestions from customers and businesses regarding new products

TIM HORTON'S

and ideas. I have however forwarded a copy of your email to the appropriate personnel for review.

Should they wish to contact you for further follow up, they have your information to do so.

Once again, thank you for contacting us and for your interest in our Company. It is through feedback from valued customers, such as yourself, that we are continually able to grow as a company.

If you have any further questions or comments please do not hesitate to contact us toll free at 1 888 601 1616.

Sincerely,
TDL Group Corp.

Kyla
Operations Service Representative

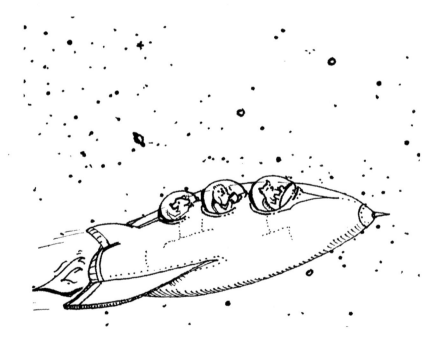

NASA

PLAN EIGHT FOR PLUTO

From: Jackson Snead
To: public-inquiries@hq.nasa.gov
Sent: Friday, August 04, 2006 2:40 PM
Subject: Plan Eight for Pluto

Dear Nasa,

I have made a rocket which I intend to pilot to
Pluto. I have spent many days looking at charts
and maps of the solar system and have pretty much
figured it out. My rocket is almost ready to go and
I have about 400 lbs of food, water and survival
gear with me.

Although it sounds like a ambitious plan, I have
been working with renowned scientist Albert
Swinehinderson and he assures me it is safe. I am

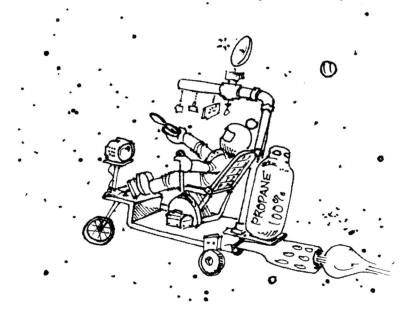

NASA

taking a GPS locator along with all the regular
instruments like a compass and a horizon ball from
an old Cessna airplane so that I can find my way
back if I get lost .

I expect to blast off next week once we get all the
tanks fueled and plan to be back for my friends
wedding in a month. I will take many photographs
which I will gladly share with you folks if you
desire. Is there anything you especially want a
photograph of?

Also, being a prudent person, I ought to do my due
diligence on Mr. Swinehinderson which includes
checking out his former job references. He has you
folks listed as his former employer and his duties
were listed as Rocket Scientist
and Navigational Specialist.   *I have a lot of*
Among his duties were designing   *money tied up in*
and aiming the rockets and he
claimed to have had successful   *propane...*
planetary bulls eyes on Mars,
Venus and Mercury but was fired for missing Uranus.

He assures me he has figured out his aiming
error and I have no worries about hitting Pluto.
(something about solar wind deflection)

Anyway, could you confirm for me that his claims
are true, as I have a lot of money tied up in propane and materials for the rocket and I would hate
to learn he was just a janitor. Still it would be
better to find out now then when I go to take off
from Pluto and find I don't have enough fuel to
make it back.

I would hate to have to call the space shuttle for
help.

158

NASA

```
Please let me know quickly, we are at T-5 days.
Jackson Snead
```

REPLY

From: HQ-Public Inquiries
To: Jackson Snead
Sent: Tuesday, August 15, 2006 10:39 AM
Subject: Unsolicited Proposal

Dear Mr. Snead:

Thank you for your inquiry to NASA. Under Federal regulation, NASA is authorized to accept technical proposals for evaluation only under one of two conditions: a proposal must either be (1) submitted in response to a formal competitive solicitation; or (2) presented as an unsolicited proposal.

The procedure for submitting an unsolicited proposal is described in a NASA guidebook located at http://ec.msfc.nasa.gov/hq/library/unSol-Prop.html. The concept you describe is not structured as an unsolicited proposal as defined by the guidebook.

Therefore, as submitted, it cannot be accepted for review. These rules are primarily intended to protect patent rights and copyright privileges of inventors.

Also, included in the above Web site are the respective NASA Centers and their particular technical areas of responsibility under the section entitled, ?NASA Research areas and addresses for submission.?

Perhaps you can address your questions directly to the respective NASA Center for an expedited response.

After you review that information, should you continue to believe

159

that your proposal would be more ap-propriately aligned with an area of re-search associated with a particular NASA Center, please forward a valid unsolicited proposal directly to that Center.

You are strongly encouraged to follow the instruc-tions as outlined in the "Guidance for the Preparations and Submission of Unsolicited Proposals," Web site so that NASA Center personnel can process and fairly review your proposal.

NASA hopes that this information will be helpful to you as you pursue your goals.   Again, thank you for your letter and interest in NASA.

Sincerely,
Public Communications and Inquiries Management Office
Office of Public Affairs

PRICELINE.COM

HOLIDAY HOBO

From: Jackson Snead
To: Priceline.com
Sent: Monday, November 07, 2005
Subject: Holiday Hobo

Category: Lowestfare Vacations
Name: Jackson Snead

Dear Priceline,

My wife and I recently returned from an exciting vacation that I think I booked through one of your affiliates in Seattle. It was an excellent time. We did a theme vacation called Holiday Hobo.

It included a freight train to Miami, 10 nights accommodation in a dumpster, an all you can eat buffet delivered to the room, dinner theatre, and a vacation pet. (I chose Rocky the Raccoon, very frisky.)

While the authentic accommodations and convincing role playing by your actors were spectacular, (Bob, the Train-yard Bull was most intimidating) I did have a hard time adjusting to the food, which arrived through the open skylight of the dumpster. I found most of the food to be excellent, but occasionally, we were served a meal that looked as though it had not been cooked at all. We usually ate it anyway as we felt that to ignore the local cuisine would be to rob ourselves of part of the experience. Speaking of robbing, the thief who showed up on the second night during dinner theatre was quite convincing. Remarkably, he stayed in character even while being taken to the hospital after misjudging the bus's stopping distance.

Either he was really injured, or he has a detachable prosthetic leg. My wife thinks it was just a dramatic plot twist to allow us to retrieve our valuables without messing up the illusion. We were so moved that we started a slow clap upon his departure. I hope you are able to pass on our most heartfelt gratitude for his dedication to his art. (I think his name was Mofo) Another notable on your staff is Gary, the patron saint of garbage, as he calls himself.

He was quite entertaining during his evening performances especially on bonfire night. Who would have thought that his beard would flame up like that with just a little spark from his cigarette? I guess there were still a lot of fumes from the spray paint lingering near his face. What a unique way of shaving. He does a pretty good break dance too. I never would have guessed that someone as old as he could spin on the top of their head while reciting

Gotta be out by noon.

PRICELINE.COM

his "magical" theories for reforming society. I think he may have injured himself one night though, as he stopped speaking for several hours and seemed to soil himself. Again though, very convincing and appropriate for the moment.

All in all it was a very wonderful and exciting adventure, and we cannot say enough good things about your organization. Many of our friends would like to go on a theme vacation like this and so we would like to book another expedition with your company. Unfortunately, the trailer where we originally booked our trip has been moved and we can't find it. Can you tell me how I can book a trip for 8 this time? We are looking at the Wilderness Wanderers of the North in the brochure. We are really looking forward to meeting Nanook of the North and his pet polar bear.We would like to leave in late January for 10 days. Please get back to me so that we can confirm our booking.

Thank you,
Jackson Snead

REPLY

From: Priceline.com
To: Jackson Snead
Sent: Wednesday, November 09, 2005
Subject: Holiday Hobo

Dear Mr. Snead,

Thank you for taking the time to send us an e-mail. We would like to help you in every way we can and understand that these are your areas of concern:

PRICELINE.COM

1. You would like to buy vacation package for Wilderness Wanderers of the North.

2. You would like to know how you can buy vacation package for a trip for 8.

1. You can view our website and find the vacation package listed on our website. In order for us to thoroughly and accurately answer your question, we invite you to please contact a Vacation Package Specialist by phone. Our specialists are available round-the-clock to help you make the best choices for your next vacation, whether it is for business or pleasure. Our knowledgeable specialists can even book your package for you, right over the phone! Please feel free to call us right away at our toll free number 1-800-658-1496.

PRICELINE.COM

We'll do our best to answer all of your questions and hopefully book you the vacation of a lifetime! We were unable to locate your previous request submitted by you with the information you provided.

Please provide as much of the following information as you can. If you have already provided some of the information, please do so again for verification. This will ensure that typing mistakes such as a missing character in your e-mail address do not prevent us from getting you the information you requested:

- Itinerary number (This is an eleven digit number) / Trip number (This is an eleven digit number)
- Account holder's name as it appears in the payment information used to make purchase
- E-mail address used to submit the request
- Date request was submitted
- FULL Names on the reservation
- Day and evening telephone numbers
- Destination - City, State, and Country
- Requested dates of travelWe will use any additional information you provide to conduct an advanced search in our database.

2. You can purchase a priceline Package in just 5 simple steps! Here's how you do it:

1. Give us the details of your trip including your departure city and desired destination, the dates you'd like to travel, the number of rooms, ages and the full names of all passengers.

2. Select the exact hotel or resort you want to stay in from our list of available locations. The prices listed for each hotel or resort include all taxes and fees.

3. Select a flight itinerary that suits you. We'll show you the cheapest flight itinerary available as part of the package price. We'll also show you other discount flight itineraries from our travel partner Lowestfare.com where you can select the airlines and flight times.

PRICELINE.COM

4. To make your package complete, you can add a rental car if your destination is within the domestic U.S. Go one step further and add Attractions and Services to make your package a unique experience.

5. Click "Buy My Package Now." Be sure to carefully review all the details of your request first and make any necessary changes. Once you purchase your package, we immediately charge the credit card you provide.

If you don't have a specific destination in mind, no problem! Use Shop by Theme to take a look at all the packages we have from all-inclusives to European getaways to Family Vacations. We thank you for the opportunity to assist you and hope this information is helpful to you.

Sincerely,
Heena R.
Customer Service Specialist

Nanook of the North and Sp'aht.

KENTUCKY FRIED CHICKEN

CLUCK 'N PLUCK MOBILE CHICKEN RESTAURANT

From: Jackson Snead
To: Kentucky Fried Chicken
Sent: Friday, August 19, 2005
Subject: Cluck'N Pluck Mobile Chicken Restaurant

Dear KFC

I am preparing to take your brand on the road. Recently, I purchased a fleet of double-decker buses which are to be mobile chicken restaurants.

This idea is an entirely fresh one and has never been done before. I am sure it will generate great publicity for you. Basically, it combines a health club and a restaurant.

The buses are designed to go to country fairs and outdoor gatherings where people will want to have some of your delicious chicken. Here is the great part of this plan. The chickens live in the upper deck of the bus. People get to go upstairs to the chicken run and catch their own dinner. That is one fun and entertaining workout.

During test marketing, there was enormous laughter as people watched the antics while patrons attempted to catch their chickens. After they catch them, the chickens are plucked and then we cook them using your special recipes. (The extra grease is recycled into diesel fuel for the bus.)

It is a great way for people to enjoy some fun, exercise and fresh, delicious chicken. It is called The KFC Cluck'N Pluck Mobile Chicken Restaurant.

KENTUCKY FRIED CHICKEN

We have 15 Buses ready to go, and all we need now
is your artwork as you would like it to appear. It
will be almost 10 ft high on the side of the bus
and very visible.

I look forward to a very enjoyable (and delicious)
future with your organization.

Thank You,
Jackson Snead

There are many advantages to keeping the chickens on the upper deck.

KENTUCKY FRIED CHICKEN

Since there was no reply from the recipients of this email, I offer the following

Manufactured Suggested Reply

Dear Mr. Snead,

Our marketing department is enthralled with the idea of creating a more interactive, healthy and fun eating environment. The fact that you are able to manufacture fuel for your getaway with the cooking drippings makes it all that more attractive.

We would like to explore the other potential benefits and features which could be derived from an operation such as yours. For instance; Could the upper chicken coop include an obstacle course to give the chickens more of a chance? Is there room for medical equipment and staff should a patron suffer a collapse during the catching part if their experience? Could you cover the bumpers in feathers to make the bus more noticeable and safe in traffic?

What about adding a few border collies just for the excitement and ambience? This could be just the break we have been looking for, putting mobile restaurants on the road and adding a workout that burns the fat as you enjoy our food.

Please go ahead and hit the road. We will be very interested in your results. Should it prove to be a popular attraction, we will gladly contribute to your corporate plan. Meanwhile, just so we don't get ahead of ourselves, could you label the bus's with a big A&W until we know for sure that you will not get sued.

BEAR MOUNTAIN RESORT

NAKED GOLFING

From: Jackson Snead
To: Bear Mountain Resort
Sent: Friday, December 2, 2005
Subject: Naked Golfing

Dear Bare Mountain

I recently heard about your development and am in charge of organizing an outing to your golf course.

I would now like to begin the process of booking my group for tee off dates and times.

I am the secretary of the Butt Shavers Nudist Club and we like to play outdoor sports in the nude. Last year we bungee jumped nude and skydived nude. This year we want to play golf. We also have an adult website that wants to broadcast the tournament on the web, this is sure to promote your development. (We have hired a bunch of Las Vegas showgirls so there will be guaranteed Hottie content.) There will be about 137 of us including; Tiger Woody, Jack Nickleass, Vijay Thingy and Annika (Big Tits) Sorenstam. We would like to play sometime this summer so there is no shrinkage. Can you tell me what dates are available?

Thank You,

Jackson Snead

BEAR MOUNTAIN RESORT

REPLY

From: Pat Buyer
To: REPLY TO ALL
Sent: Friday, December 9, 2005
Subject: Bear Mountain Resort

What do you make of this one?

> From: Jackson Snead
> Sent: Friday, December 2, 2005
> To: Pat Buyer; Betty Novak
> Subject: Resort Contact Form Submission
>
> Dear Bare Mountain
>
> I recently heard about your development and am in charge
> of organizing an outing to your golf course. I would now like
> to begin the process of booking my group for tee off dates
> and times. I am the secretary of the Butt Shavers Nudist
> Club and we like to play outdoor sports in the nude. Last
> year we bungee jumped nude and skydived nude. This year
> we want to play golf. We also have an adult website that
> wants to broadcast the tournament on the web, this is sure to
> promote your development. (We have hired a bunch of Las
> Vegas showgirls so there will be guaranteed Hottie content.)
> There will be about 137 of us including; Tiger Woody, Jack
> Nickleass, Vijay Thingy and Annika (Big Tits) Sorenstam.
> We would like to play sometime this summer so there is no
> shrinkage. Can you tell me what dates are available?
>
> Thank You,
> Jackson Snead

Pat Buyer
Director of Resort Sales

BEAR MOUNTAIN RESORT

From: Pat Buyer
To: Jackson Snead
Sent: Wednesday, December 14, 2005
Subject: Bear Mountain Resort

Dear Mr. Snead,

Thank you for considering Bear Mountain Resort for your summer outing. Unfortunately I do not feel that we are the appropriate destination for your event, as there are several houses built along the golf course, of which there are several children. While it is not my intent to pass judgement on the nature of your activities, I am sure there are several parents within the community who would object to the event taking place on a public golf course.

Again, thank you for your consideration. Please feel free to contact me again if I can be of any further assistance.

Kind regards,

Pat Buyer

Director of Resort Sales

Skins game...

ENQUIRY BC

WHO DO I REPORT THIS TO?

From: Jackson Snead
To: Enquiry BC
Sent: Tuesday, January 10, 2006
Subject: Who do I report this to?

Dear Sirs,

If it turns out that I happen to know where a bigfoot is, who would I report it to?

Jackson Snead

REPLY

From: "Enquiry BC
To: Jackson Snead
Sent: Wednesday, January 11, 2006
Subject: RE: Who do I report this to?

Thank you for your enquiry. You may wish to forward your e-mail to the Correspondence Unit of the Ministry of Environment at: env.minister@gov.bc.ca, as they may be able to assist you. Alternately, you may wish to contact the Conservation Officer Services of the Ministry of Environment.

You may wish to call toll free at: 1-(800) 663-9453, 24 hours. You may wish to visit the web site at: http://wlapwww.gov.bc.ca/cos/index. htm. Unfortunately, the office does not have a direct e-mail address.

ENQUIRY BC CALL CENTRE
Hours of Operation: 7:30am to 5pm, Mon- Friday, except statutories.
In Vancouver 604/660-2421
In Victoria 250/387-6121 Elsewhere in BC 1-800/663-7867 (toll free)

BC MINISTRY OF ENVIRONMENT

MY BROTHER IS A BIGFOOT

From: Jackson Snead
To: Ministry of Environment
Sent: Thursday, January 12, 2006
Subject: My Brother is a Bigfoot

Dear Ministry of the Environment,

I have been holding a secret for many years and I now am ready to spill the beans.

My brother is bigfoot! I wasn't going to say anything, but he owes me money and wrecked my car again and he really pissed me off and he is not

being responsible so I feel I have to blow the whistle.

It has been a family secret for 24 years since we found him under a stump near Sombrio beach. At the time, we were just going to turn him over to welfare, but they didn't believe us and told us it was not in their jurisdiction since he wasn't actually human.

We also contacted several wildlife agencies but they wouldn't send anyone around, so we just shaved him and kept him. He looks like a really big, ugly human but I could just be biased. (I think my sister is kind of froggy too.) He has always borrowed money off me since he has a hard time keeping a job. (Most uniforms do not fit him, he is seven feet tall and has all that back hair.) It's been almost a year since I got a payment from him and then he wrecked the car on the weekend. I

BC MINISTRY OF ENVIRONMENT

told him I would tell if he didn't pay me, but he doesn't care. He said he would just blend in with the forest when you come around to get him. If you

want to make it easy to pick him up, I can tell you where he will be on next Monday morning. (I ordered a few goats and he never misses goat day.)

I do have a couple questions though before I set him up for your agents,

1) Is there any reward for turning in a bigfoot?

2) If you put him in a zoo or something will he get paid or can you pay me? (At least till he pays off my car.)

3) How much would you pay him?

3) If he does get put in a zoo, does he get out on holidays?

4). Will you be teaching him any new tricks? He already knows how to juggle.

5) Will he be able to keep his cell phone?

Please get back to me quickly so I can confirm the goat delivery day.

Jackson Snead

Shaving baby Bigfoot

175

BC MINISTRY OF ENVIRONMENT

Since there was no reply from the recipients of this email, I offer the following

Manufactured Suggested Reply

Dear Mr. Snead

We received your email regarding the bigfoot which you claim to have grown up with. Please document your experiences in our Wildlife Form 213-B and explain in detail the efforts made to return the animal to the wilds. You must also fill out form BF-ICU-1 detailing where and when you first spotted Bigfoot. Also, please fill out form 657-AZ-86 which deals with the amount of penalty you face for unauthorized imprisonment of a wild creature.

We also require that you provide documentation of the types of food provided, how its waste was disposed of and where we might find its waste products.

Should it be determined that they are toxic waste products, you will have to fill out form 666-FYAL-9 which determines the amount of fines you face for improper disposal of toxic wastes.

Finally we have form 885-G which deals with unlicensed wild animals on private property and the amount of fines applicable.

Should you find all this daunting and overwhelming, you are invited to call our auditor who will assess the applicable charges for you including the costs for future care of the bigfoot in our facility.

Perhaps this is why we have never actually found a Bigfoot.

BC PREMIERS OFFICE

MY BROTHER IS A BIGFOOT

From: Jackson Snead
To: BC Premier's Office
Sent: Tuesday, January 17, 2006
Subject: My Brother is a Bigfoot

Dear Mr. Premier,

I don't expect you to do anything about this, but I just want you to know what's going on in your province.

Originally, I had informed welfare of this  situation and they said it was not their jurisdiction. Then I wrote the Ministry of Environment last week to inform them, but they just ignored me, so I thought I would tell you.

Here goes: my brother is a Bigfoot. We found him many years ago under a stump on Sombrio Beach and since no one would take him off our hands, we just shaved him and kept him. Today he is about seven feet tall with long brown hair and is a high school graduate. (He  won't shave anymore.) When I told you folks about him last week, I thought that you would arrive at our door within minutes, but it seems that nobody really cares. For 24 years now, we have been dressing him and brushing him and teaching him proper table manners in the hopes of having him blend in with society, all the while keeping him in line with the threat of revealing him to the

177

BC PREMIERS OFFICE

authorities and then it turns out to be a totally
empty threat. What do you think he learns from
that? I also thought that I might get some sort of
reward for taking care of him all these years and
turning him in, but that seems fairly unlikely now.

Don't get me wrong, I really like my brother and I
wasn't going to report him, but he owes me a lot of
money and he wrecked my car again and he won't get
another job to pay for it. He needs to be taught
a lesson. If he were a responsible guy who just
needed a break, no problem, but he seems to think
that the world owes him a living. He has a really
bad work ethic. His idea of hard work is hiding
behind a tree and not being seen. Unfortunately,
at most jobs you can only hide
behind so many things before you

start to get a reputation. I must
say though, he is pretty good at
hiding. (World champion 1997-98)

So anyway, if I
can't get him arrested, I might
as well get him a job so that
he can pay me back. Do you know
of any kind of job that might
be available for him where his
natural talents would be appreciated? He's quite
big and smelly and speaks with an accent but other
then that, he's pretty normal. (Except for all the
hair and being real ugly too.) How about if he was
a goodwill ambassador. I'll bet having a Bigfoot
meet & greet would be a big draw. Hey, do you think
he could run for office? I think he's a Liberal.

Thanks
Jackson Snead

BC PREMIERS OFFICE

Since there was no reply from the recipients of this email, I offer the following

Manufactured Suggested Reply

Dear Mr. Snead

Thank you for your kind offer to provide your brother the bigfoot as my running mate in the next election. I expect this will be a very good strategy. I can make him a minister of everything and if something goes wrong, I can blame him. Given his hiding skills, he is eminently qualified for a government position.

I am sure he will be the greatest scapegoat ever.

Honorably,
The Premier of British Columbia

SANTA CLAUS

MY BROTHER IS A BIGFOOT

From: Jackson Snead
To: Santa
Sent: Sunday, Dec 18, 2005
Subject: My Brother is a Bigfoot

Dear Santa,

Let's say, hypothetically, that my brother is a bigfoot. Who should I report him to?

Jackson Snead

REPLY

From: Santa
To: Jackson Snead
Sent: Monday, Dec 19, 2005
Subject: My Brother is a Bigfoot

Hello There Jackson Snead and a very Merry Christmas to you!

What a wonderful and magical time of year this is! I am almost ready for my journey around the world delivering gifts to good boys and girls everywhere. The reindeer are chomping at the bit and can't wait to take flight. All the elves have prepared the sleigh with lots of gifts, and Mrs. Claus has made me a special batch of her cookies. Mmmm Yummy!

Make sure you get to bed early on Christmas Eve and don't forget I love those cookies. I hope everyone is thankful for what they have, and I hope everyone will do their best to help those less fortunate in the coming year.

SANTA CLAUS

From Santa, Mrs. Claus, the elves and the reindeer...

A Very Merry Christmas and a Happy New Year!

Santa Claus.

P.S. Now there are two ways to see how close Santa is to your house on Christmas Eve. There's the Santa Spotter on Claus.com at http://www.claus.com/spotter/index.php. Plus, Santa now has a phone in his sleigh, so he can talk to children around the world during his flight. Parents can see the details if they go to http://www.claus.com and click on the red phone booth in the village

Santa says, "Bigfoot Babies make excellent stocking stuffers."

ANDORRAN EMBASSY

I'D LIKE TO JOIN THE OLYMPIC TEAM

From: Jackson Snead
To: Andorran Embassy
Sent: Monday, December 15, 2003
Subject: I'd Like To Join The Olympic Team

Dear Sirs.

I am writing to you because I have to start somewhere. I hope you can direct me where to write, and I will describe my situation as best as possible.

I have a proud Andorran ancestry on my mother's side and am looking to reconnect with my heritage. My great grandfather emigrated many years ago in search of greener pastures (he was a shepherd) and ended up in Canada. Although I have never been to Andorra, I still feel a kinship to it and would like to do something for the nation.

...as long as I don't open my eyes, I am sure that I would not scream.

It occurred to me that since the Olympics are being held in Vancouver in 2010, not to far away from where I currently live, is there a possibility that I could join the Andorran winter Olympic team?

I'm not that great at skiing or endurance, but I can slide downhill pretty good, so I thought that the perfect opening for me would be as the 3rd man on the 4-man bobsled team. I don't want to steer, or be the last one on board, (phobias about being left behind) but I'm good at keeping my head down, and as long as I don't open my eyes, I am sure that I would not scream.

182

ANDORRAN EMBASSY

I think that my
lack of skill
or experience
can be made up
for by the fact
that I am very
enthusiastic
and live pretty
close to Whistler
Mountain. I could
meet the team
there, so there
would be no need
to pay for any
expensive flights
or transportation
for me.

I'm also a
vegetarian, so
you know the
meal costs will
be minimal. No
fillet mignon for
me.

I hope you look
favorably on
this request and
are able to pass it on to the person or committee
responsible. I look forward to a proud moment atop
the medal podium.

Sincerely, Jackson Snead

P.S. Do you know where I can get a recording of the
Andorran national anthem?

ANDORRAN EMBASSY

REPLY

Since there was no reply from the recipients of this email, I offer the following

Manufactured Suggested Reply

Dear Mr. Snead
It looks like you are going downhill way faster than anyone else could ever hope to attain. Should we launch any type of downhill sliding team, you will be first on our list.

LEE VALLEY TOOLS

STUD FINDER

From: Jackson Snead
To: Lee Valley Tools
Sent: Sunday, January 19, 2003
Subject: Stud finder

Dear Robin

Since you are one of the premier wood working tool distributors in the world, I thought I would run a product idea by you. My head is the ultimate stud finder.

If I am walking in a basement with a low ceiling, you can bet dollars to donuts that my noggin will end up finding the thickest piece of wood in the basement. It happens in the attic too. I can be crawling around, not necessarily looking for anything, when WHAM, my head will end up against a rafter.

This may not be a unique ability, as when I tell my friends of my special talent, they proclaim to have elements of the same powers, although it manifests in a slightly different manner. (For example, Judy attracts alcoholics.)

Stud Finder with audible signal.

185

LEE VALLEY TOOLS

But we tested it in laboratory conditions, and out of over 16 people, I was the only one that consistently ended up against a piece of wood.

So I have definite proof that my bones attract studs, rafters, joists and thick wood. It especially applies to my skull.

My question to you, (before I go and blow a bunch of money on cloning my head) is, would you people be interested in marketing a new kind of stud finder? It might look like me, so it should be fairly attractive, and it gives an audible signal when it finds a stud.

Full of Ideas,
Jackson Snead

REPLY

From: Lee Valley Tools
To: Jackson Snead
Sent: Tuesday, January 21
Subject: Stud Finder

Jackson -

I already have a good stud finder - attractive, and gives audible signals - my wife... she found me, didn't she?

Cheers,

Rob Lee

C. Stud Finder

This is one of our most popular stud finders, with gold band and 10 carat stone. Girls, if you see one of these, you have found yourself a stud.

186

ESSO

PUMP ME UP

From: Jackson Snead
To: Esso Oil
Sent: Saturday, July 08, 2006 1:48 PM
Subject: Pump Me Up

Dear Exxon

I have used your gas exclusively in my cars for the
last 30 years, ever since a very kind Esso employee prevented me from using the wrong fuel to start
my bar-b-que and probably saved my dog and myself
from a potentially disastrous 4th of July party.
I am probably one of those rare people who think
Exxon earns their keep in our society by providing
the fuel that drives our civilization.

Those that say gas is to expensive should go out
and make it themselves. I say we are getting a
bargain, even if it rose to $10.00 a gallon.

Recently, I have
begun using the
pay at the pump
feature at your
stations given
the time con-
straints placed
on your employees
and their limited
time to shoot
the breeze.

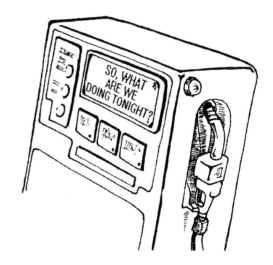

I was therefore
quite happy when

187

ESSO

the question screen on the pump began asking more personalized questions. I think that is the next logical step to bringing back a little personality to your stations and I applaud your innovation.

I must admit though, the first time it happened, I was a bit shocked, but it was an innocent enough banter, just "Do you like the weather today?" Press YES/NO. Then it was stuff like, "Do you like the feel of my pump handle?" Press YES/NO.

I guess this is your way of doing customer research. Pretty soon though, various pumps had started to develop a personality through their inquiries. I knew some would ask about the weather, others about the car, but still another asked me my phone number.

I punched in my phone number but as yet I have not had a phone call from your organization. Do you think I can expect a phone call from one of your reps to chat at some point. I realize that during the business day the employees may be to busy, but after hours would be OK by me.

Thanks
Jackson Snead

ESSO

REPLY

From: ESSO
To: Jackson Snead
Sent: Friday, July 07, 2006 3:02 PM
Subject: Re: Pumps
Re: File # 860662

Dear Mr. Snead,

Thank you for taking the time to contact Imperial Oil. Imperial Oil and Esso-branded retailers are committed to providing our customers with quality products and hassle-free customer service. To help us address your concerns, please respond with the following information:
* The date and time of your visit:
 * The pump number, or brief description of its location:
 * Your loyalty number (Speedpass, Esso Extra or Aeroplan):
 * Your current mailing address and telephone number:
Please confirm if you were at an Esso branded service station and if the location was at 3954 Shelbourne Street in Victoria.

Thank you once again for taking the time to contact us, and allowing us the opportunity to address this matter.

Sincerely,
Joe Gibbs
Customer Service Specialist
www.essoextra.com
www.speedpass.ca

Note: When responding to this message, please use reply to keep the email thread intact. We need to see the information on previous e-mails to better assist you.

ESSO

REPLY

From: Jackson Snead
To: Esso Oil
Sent: Wednesday, July 12, 2006
Subject: Pump Me Up

Dear Joe,

No need to thank me for contacting you guys, I have always enjoyed talking to gasoline people. I guess you guys are really busy right now given all the gas you have to make and deliver. I do appreciate you taking an interest in me but I don't know if I can answer all your questions. First of all, I didn't know the pumps had numbers, and I didn't think to ask when it asked for mine.

As far as location, they were all right out in front of the garage, mounted in the middle of the driveway with a little roof over them. I go to an Esso about every week if I am driving a lot, and I just seem to find them all over the place.

I have been to the Shelbourne Esso though, and it's a very nice one. I'm afraid I don't have any special loyalty number, but I would say I'm your number one fan. I sure like the new questions being asked by your pumps. It makes me feel valued.

ESSO

Yesterday, a pump asked me if I had ever blown a gasket. This reminded me to change my oil, which I did. A few weeks ago, another asked me if I had rock hard abs, so I checked my brakes.

(I was low on fluid so it was a good tip) I might have had a brake failure if not for the pump. It's very nice to be treated with such special care when I come into your stations, and the questions just help to remind me of all the little things I tend to forget.

It sure helps to make up for all the impersonal service we tend to get at larger institutions these days.

I'd be happy to give you my phone number, it's 250-XXX-2635, what's yours Joe? Currently I'm staying at the West Bay RV park, pad 42. It has a great view of Victoria's harbor and I sure liked the fireworks this year.

Did you guys have good fireworks where you are?

Thanks,

Jackson

DUCKS UNLIMITED

STOP THE FENCE!

Dear Ducks Unlimited,

I heard recently about the US proposal to install fences along their southern border to stop aliens from gaining entry. Apparently this is to be a 700 mile fence.

Now, I don't know if this is inspired by those Mexican UFO videos that we saw on TV a few years ago or if it is just another protectionist plot on their part, but what I do know is that a 700 mile high fence will disrupt the migratory patterns of most birds and do nothing to stop the aliens from either going around and approaching by sea or coming from space.

I think this is some kind of plot by fence manufacturer's lobbyists who have an interest in selling lots of fencing material.

In any case, can I count on Ducks unlimited to mobilize their vast network of conservationists to help stop this insane project which will surely disrupt migratory patterns and thus endanger many species of birds which are unable to achieve the required altitude?

Jackson Snead

DUCKS UNLIMITED

REPLY

From: Webfoot
To: Jackson Snead
Sent: Friday, June 16, 2006 11:50 AM
Subject: RE: Stop The Fence

Dear Jackson,

Thank you for contacting Ducks Unlimited Canada, Canada's Conservation Company. Your email of June 15th regarding a fence has been forwarded to the appropriate area.

We thank you for taking the time to communicate with us and please feel free to contact us should you require further information.

Sincerely,

Debbie Menard

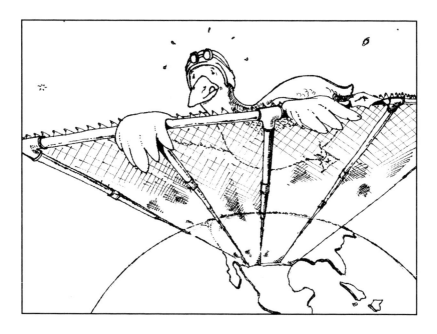

LABATTS

BEER'S BEST FRIEND

From: Jackson Snead
To: Labatt's Brewery
Sent: Friday, June 23 , 2006 11:27 AM
Subject: Beer's Best Friend

Dear Sirs

Recently I heard that your company was going to bring out a new kind of beer container that was designed like a bowl with a pull-off top for dogs to drink from.

I am anxious to see this appear on the market as my dog has a hard time drinking from regular cans and bottles. I would welcome having an instant dog beer bowl when I go camping and such. As it is now, I have to dump his water and the pour in beer and if he then wants water, I have to dump the beer, or I have to hold the can or bottle for him. Its really inconvenient.

It would be great to be able to pop one open for Rover as we sit around the campfire and just let him enjoy drinking at his own pace.

Please let me know when you expect to launch this great new product.

Thanks,

Jackson Snead

PS. If you think we are best friends now, just wait till we go on a couple of benders together!!!

194

LABATTS

REPLY

From: Labatt's Brewery
To: Jackson Snead ;
Sent: Friday, June 30, 2006 10:54 AM
Subject: RE: Beer's Best Friend

Thank you for your email Jackson.
Unfortunately, I've never heard of this
new product. Is it possible for you to
send more details so we may look into this further? Did you see this
product in a commercial? What brand of beer was it advertising?

Best regards,
Yvette
Labatt Breweries

REPLY

From: Jackson Snead
To: Labatt's Brewery ;
Sent: Friday, June 30, 2006 11:35 AM
Subject: RE: Beer's Best Friend

Dear Yvette,

Thanks for getting back to me so quickly. I think I
saw this advertised during a football game. There
was a bunch of dogs sitting
around playing poker lapping it
up. A Collie, a Boxer, a German
Shepherd, a St. Bernard, and a
Schnauzer. (A Basset hound was
serving snacks.)

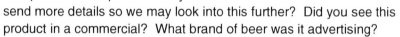

LABATTS

It came with a free pack of cards and some Milk-
bones. It was a great commercial. I think the tag
line was "Lappin' up Labatts." The dogs were having
a very good time, although the Schnauzer seemed to
be a little surley. (Maybe he was losing)Anyway,
if you do make this, put me down for a couple of
cases. Rover has taken to crushing his empties,
behavior I would like to discourage, and I will
when he starts getting the Beer-bowl. That sucker
looked pretty sturdy. We can probably use it to
cook in when the beer is gone.

Thanks for keeping me in the loop,
Jackson

REPLY

From: Labatt's Brewery
To: Jackson Snead ;
Sent: Monday, July 3, 2006 10:54 AM
Subject: RE: Beer's Best Friend

Hi Jackson,

I believe that you are referring to the ad below. We do not have
this product on market . Please be aware that this is not one of

our Web Site, however
you are more than
welcome to check out the
following website 'www.
beerfordogs.com'.

Cheers!
Katherine
Labatt Customer Service

196

CITY CONFERENCE CENTRE

INTERNATIONAL ASSOCIATION OF INDOOR AQUARIUM FARMERS

From: Jackson Snead
To: Alice Winters, City Conference Center
Sent: Monday, December 05, 2005 6:25 PM
Subject: International Association of Indoor
Aquarium Farmers

Dear Alice Winters,

I am doing some preparation for our group and have been asked to investigate your facility.

Next year we are considering hosting the worldwide convention of The International Association of Indoor Aquarium Farmers (IAIAF) in your city. We need to rent an exhibition hall where we can gather, exhibit our fish and aquariums, give out awards, and party, party, party.

We have a wide range of interesting and spectacular exhibits to display and we have some questions regarding your policies. We need to set up approximately 45 large aquariums, as well as one of the world's largest

Homesteading pioneer aquarium farmers Rebecca and Joshua with some of the tools of their trade.

CITY CONFERENCE CENTRE

portable dolphin tanks. Can you tell me what kind of floor covering you have in the large exhibition hall, and is it waterproof?

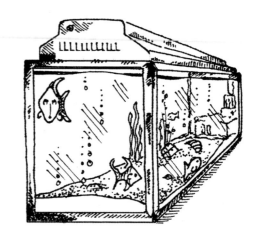

I also need to know how high the ceiling is. (For the safety of the dolphins.) There are several exhibits that give off odors. Can you tell me the CFM of your air exchange system?

Is open flame allowed at your facility?

Can we supply our own chefs to create the new recipes for the enjoyment of our members? Are there any laws restricting the ingestion of live fish in your city? (We have a swallowing contest; Goldfish and Neon Tetras, maybe a small Mackerel, definitely no Dolphins)

There will be about 250 of us and rather then rent over 100 rooms, some of us would like to sleep in the main exhibition hall on foam mattress's or cots? Would that be extra?

Please get back to me quickly so that we may adequately prepare for our exhibition.

Thank You,
Jackson Snead

CITY CONFERENCE CENTRE

REPLY

From: Alice Winters, City Conference Center
To: Jackson Snead
Sent: Tuesday, December 06, 2005 9:10 AM
Subject: RE: International Association of Indoor Aquarium Farmers

Hello Jackson,

Thanks for you message. I would like to learn more about your organization before we move forward. Does the IAIAF have a web site? Where has the convention been held in the past?

Best Regards,
Alice Winters
Account Executive

REPLY

From: Jackson Snead
To: Alice Winters, City Conference Center
Sent: Tuesday, December 06, 2005 12:24 PM
Subject: Re: International Association of Indoor Aquarium Farmers

Hi Alice,

Thanks for your quick reply, Sorry to say we do not have a website yet and this is only our second convention. The last one we had was in Pomeratu three years ago. We were formed to encourage third world groups and shut-ins to make use of the available food sources in their aquariums and develop other aquaculture initiatives. It is the most efficient use of aquaculture technology on the

CITY CONFERENCE CENTRE

planet and we are very excited about the potential.

We recently received some funding from the U.N. which allows us to regroup and afford another convention. We expect to spend roughly $350,000.00 during our three day event.

Unfortunately, we had to ban the delegates from Nunavut as a precautionary measure this year. (Bad for them, good for you. You really don't want to have a demonstration of whale hunting and filleting in your convention center. Besides, it is really  not a practical aquarium so it does not fit our mandate.) We have had some stunning developments in the last few years and you will be amazed at what can be harvested from a regular aquarium. One of our professors, Albert Swinehinderson has been subsisting for an entire year on the harvest he gains from a series of aquariums in his basement.

He is our keynote speaker and will appear on our poster. He has distinctive hair, so you will recognize him when you see him; he has been on TV a lot lately.

As mentioned, we expect about 250 people from all over the world and all kinds of interesting exhibits. I hope you will be able to take a cruise through the exhibits and maybe you too will join our group. Did you know that you can feed a family of four with only nine 30 gallon aquariums? We also hope to charge admission for the general public. Does this fit with your policies?

Jackson Snead

CITY CONFERENCE CENTRE

REPLY

From: Alice Winters, City Conference Center
To: Jackson Snead
Sent: Wednesday, December 07, 2005 11:27 AM
Subject: RE: International Association of Indoor Aquarium Farmers

Hello again Jackson,

I need to do some further research before I can answer some of your questions regarding water exhibits and fish activities. I will get back to you in the next day or so. In the meantime, can you please tell me what dates you are considering for 2006?

Thanks again for your message.
Alice Winters
Account Executive

From: Alice Winters, City Conference Center
To: Jackson Snead
Sent: Wednesday, December 07, 2005 11:38 AM
Subject: RE: International Association of Indoor Aquarium Farmers

Hello again Jackson,

Just a quick note to let you know that I did some further research and won't be able to follow up on your request, especially since you are "currently the living God of Pomeratu, an Island in the south Pacific inhabited by a cargo cult" (jacksonsnead.blogspot.com). We do not work with people associated with cults.

Best Regards,
Alice Winters

FINIS

ISBN 141208444-X